INTRODUCTION

MY NAME IS NICOLE M. KLOTTER, AND I WOULD LIKE TO SHARE SOME VERY PERSONAL STUFF ABOUT MYSELF. YOU'RE PROBABLY WONDERING WHY YOU WOULD WANT TO READ ABOUT ME, BUT THIS ISN'T ALL ABOUT ME. IT IS ABOUT MAKING A DIFFERENCE IN THE JUSTICE SYSTEM. TO GET HELP WITHOUT JUDGEMENT AND TO BETTER THE LIVES OF SO MANY PEOPLE.

NOW I AM AN ADDICT AND ALSO SUFFER FROM MENTAL HEALTH ISSUES. I AM ALSO CURRENTLY INCARCERATED AS I WRITE THIS BOOK. I HAVE BEEN INCARCERATED SINCE 4-20-2009 AND WILL REMAIN SO UNTIL 4-20-2019. I WILL SHARE WITH YOU "WHY" LATER ON. I AM 41 YEARS OLD FOR THE FIRST TIME I CAN HONESTLY SAY WHO I AM AND BE PROUD OF WHO I AM.

I WOULD ALSO LIKE TO SHARE SOME PERSONAL STORIES WITH YOU, FROM OTHER INMATES WHO STRUGGLE WITH ADDICTIONS AND MENTAL HEALTH ISSUES, AND A LOT OF TRAUMA AND ABUSE, VIEWS FROM MANY SOCIAL WORKERS, PSYCHOLOGISTS AND MANY OTHERS.

THE GOAL I HAVE FOR THIS BOOK IS TO MAKE PEOPLE AWARE OF THE STRUGGLES THAT MEN AND WOMEN FACE ON A DAILY BASIS DUE TO ADDICTIONS AND MENTAL HEALTH ISSUES. LIKE I SAID IN THE BEGINNING, MY MAIN GOAL IS TO MAKE A DIFFERENCE!!

I HOPE THAT THIS BOOK WILL BRING ABOUT CHANGE IN OUR COMMUNITY. HELP PEOPLE TO NOTICE WHAT IS GOING ON IN OUR COMMUNITY. HELP THEM TO UNDERSTAND WHY INCARCERATION IS NOT ALWAYS THE ANSWER TO SITUATIONS.

I HOPE PEOPLE WILL SEE HOW KINDNESS IS IMPORTANT AND NOT JUDGEMENTS. HOW WE AS A COMMUNITY CAN MAKE A DIFFERENCE EVEN IF IT IS IN ONE PERSONS LIFE. ENJOY READING THIS BOOK AND MAY GOD BLESS YOU IN YOUR OWN JOURNEY THROUGH THIS LIFE. WE ALL STRUGGLE AND WE ALL NEED UNDERSTANDING AND KINDNESS IN OUR LIVES. I HOPE THIS BOOK FULFILLS THAT FOR YOU.

THANK YOU!

NICOLE M. KLOTTER

ACHKNOWLEDGEMENTS

THIS PAGE IS VERY NEAR AND DEAR TO MY HEART BECAUSE THERE ARE SO MANY PEOPLE RESPONSIBLE FOR THIS BOOK! WITHOUT THE ENCOURAGEMENT, SUPPORT, AND FAITH THAT ALL THESE PEOPLE SHOWED ME THIS BOOK WOULD HAVE NEVER HAPPENED! I WANT TO THANK YOU ALL FOR EVERYTHING! MY LIFE HAS CHANGED IN SO MANY WAYS BECAUSE OF YOU! THANK YOU! YOU ARE ALL LOVED, APPRECIATED, AND THOUGHT OF FONDLY.

FIRST, THERE IS MEGAN THUMANN FOR DEALING WITH ME WHEN NO ONE ELSE WOULD. FOR ENCOURAGING ME AND HELPING ME TO SEE THAT THE ABUSE I ENDURED WAS NOT MY FAULT. THAT I HAD THE STRENGTH TO MAKE CHANGES SO THAT I COULD HAVE A BRIGHTER FUTURE! THE STRENGTH TO HELP OTHERS AND THE COURAGE TO SHARE MY STORY!

CHAD, WHAT CAN I SAY ABOUT YOU? YOU WENT THROUGH HELL WITH ME AND BACK AGAIN MANY TIMES. YOU SAW ME AT MY WORST. FIGHTING, SWEARING, BEING VERBALLY ABUSED, NO SELF-ESTEEM, NO SELF-CONFIDENCE, MEANNESS, NO INTEGRITY, YOU NAME IT YOU SAW IT AND YET YOU STILL BELIEVED IN ME! AT FIRST, I DID NOT BELIEVE A WORD YOU SAID BUT YOUR ACTIONS JUST KEPT CHIPPING AWAY AT MY BARRIERS! YOU ROCK! THOSE LADIES THAT ARE IN YOUR CARE DO NOT KNOW HOW LUCKY THEY TRULY ARE TO HAVE YOU IN THEIR CORNER!! THANK YOU AND I AM SO SORRY FOR ALL THE ABUSE I PUT YOU THROUGH! THANK YOU FOR STANDING BY ME AND BELIEVING IN ME!

ASHLEY EVERS, EVERY TIME I THINK ABOUT YOU, I MUST LAUGH, BECAUSE YOU REALLY HAD YOUR HANDS FULL WITH ME. WHEN I FIRST MET YOU, I DID NOT LIKE YOU. I THOUGHT YOU WERE JUST SOME YOUNG WOMAN TRYING TO GET BY AND SPOUT A BUNCH OF CRAP, BUT YOU PROVED ME COMPLETELY WRONG. WHEN I FIRST STARTED THIS BOOK, YOU HAD NO DOUBTS IN ME, YOU JUST WENT TO WORK HELPING ME RESEARCH WHAT I NEEDED. THANK YOU. THANK YOU FOR JUST BEING YOU. THANK YOU FOR YOUR KINDNESS WHEN I DID NOT DESERVE KINDNESS AND THANK YOU FOR ALWAYS KEEPING IT REAL WITH ME! I APPRECIATE THAT MOST OF ALL. MY FAITH IN PEOPLE WAS NIL, BUT YOU KEPT BEING REAL EVEN WHEN I CALLED YOU A LIAR AND FLAT OUT SAID I DID NOT BELIEVE YOU! THANK YOU SO MUCH.

SARAH PULS! WHAT CAN I SAY EXCEPT I AM SORRY AND THANK YOU! LOL YOU HAVE THE STRENGTH OF TEN MULES AFTER DEALING WITH ME! YOU ENCOURAGED ME, CHASTISED ME, SET ME STRAIGHT AND WHEN I TOLD YOU I WANTED TO SHARE MY STORY YOU NEVER DOUBTED ME! YOU HAD SO MUCH ON YOUR PLATE, AND I JUST ADDED TO IT AND I AM SORRY. THANK YOU FOR YOUR COMPASSION. YOUR KINDNESS. YOUR STRENGTH. YOUR FAITH. YOUR ENCOURAGEMENT. YOU ROCK!

TAMRA OMAN, GIIIIIRLLL! YOU ARE SOMETHING ELSE! I COULD WRITE A WHOLE BOOK ON WHAT YOU HAVE DONE FOR ME! LOL. WHEN I FIRST MET YOU, I DID NOT LIKE YOU ONE IOTA. I THOUGHT YOU WERE LOUD, OBNOXIOUS, AND FULL OF S**T. THEN I LISTENED TO YOUR STORY AND STARTED TO WONDER ABOUT YOU. WONDER ABOUT THIS WOMAN YOU HAD CLAIMED TO BECOME. I REALLY STARTED TO SCRUTINIZE YOUR EVERY MOVE. LOOKING FOR THAT ONE LIE. NEVER CAME. YOUR WORD MEANT SOMETHING TO YOU. THEN I STARTED TO RESPECT YOU. I KNEW WHAT YOU SAID HAD TO BE TRUE BECAUSE YOUR ACTIONS ALWAYS BACKED THEM UP. THEN ONE DAY YOU AND I SAT IN THE PING PONG ROOM AND I REALIZED WHY I DID NOT LIKE YOU AT FIRST. YOU AND I WERE SO SIMILAR. IT SCARED ME. LOOKING AT YOU I SAW THAT I COULD NOT HAVE EXCUSES. I COULD MAKE SOMETHING OUT OF MY LIFE. ONCE I GOT OUT OF PRISON YOU BECAME MY FRIEND, MY MENTOR, MY SISTER. I LOVE YOU SISTER! GOD IS USING YOU IN INCREDIBLE WAYS. THANK YOU FOR ALWAYS BELIEVING IN ME, FOR NEVER BEING SCARED TO PUT ME IN MY SPACE YET HAVING TOTAL COMPASSION FOR MY SITUATION. THANK YOU FOR ALL YOUR HELP!

SHERRY HUNTER-LOL- PEOPLE TALK MAJOR CRAP ABOUT THEIR PROBATION OFFICERS, I CANNOT! YOU BELIEVE IN ME AND YOU TREAT ME LIKE A HUMAN. YOU SHOW ME EVERYDAY TRUST AND FAITH THAT I DESERVE TODAY. WHEN I FIRST MET YOU, YOU DID NOT TREAT ME LIKE A COMMON CRIMINAL, BUT YOU WERE TOUGH AT FIRST. ONCE I PROVED MYSELF TO YOU, I KNEW I HAD GAINED YOUR RESPECT AND THAT MEANS THE WORLD TO ME. THANK YOU FOR SHOWING ME THAT I AM STRONG AND CAN DO ANYTHING I PUT MY MIND TO. THANK YOU FOR ALWAYS TREATING ME LIKE A HUMAN BEING. FOR ALWAYS LOOKING OUT FOR ME AND MY MENTAL HEALTH ISSUES. THIS JOURNEY WOULD BE IMPOSSIBLE WITHOUT YOU!

BLAINE KING! I LOVE YOU! DESPITE ALL THE PROBLEMS, UPHEAVALS, ARGUMENTS, BREAK UPS, UPS AND DOWNS YOU REMAIN MY ABSOLUTE BEST FRIEND, MY BIGGEST SUPPORTER IN ALL THINGS AND MOST OF ALL MY BIGGEST CHAMPION! YOU HAVE ALWAYS SUPPORTED ME IN ANYTHING I EVER WANTED TO DO OR NOT DO.

SAVANNAH KING! I LOVE YOU. YOU ARE MY DAUGHTER AND NOTHING IN THIS WORLD WILL EVER CHANGE THAT. YOU MAY NOT BE MINE BIOLOGICALLY, BUT YOU ARE MY LIFE, MY WORLD, MY EVERYTHING, AND I AM SO PROUD TO CALL YOU....MY DAUGHTER!!!

TO MY CHILDREN THAT I DID GIVE BIRTH TO, WHO HATE ME AND FEEL LIKE I AM NOTHING, JUST KNOW I AM SOMETHING! I SCREWED UP A LOT IN MY LIFE, I STRUGGLE, BUT WHO I WAS 15,20,30 YEARS AGO IS NOT WHO I AM TODAY. ALL OF YOU ARE MISSING OUT ON A GREAT

MOTHER WHO HAS HAD TO OVERCOME MANY OBSTACLES IN HER LIFE. YOU ARE MISSING OUT ON A GREAT LOVE! I LOVE YOU ALL AND THAT WILL NEVER CHANGE! ONE DAY YOU WILL SEE WHAT YOU ARE MISSING OUT ON AND I WILL BE THERE WITH OPEN ARMS!

CHAPTER ONE

Addiction and Me

This chapter will lead us to a lot of the different addictions and how people got there. Many times, in life I prayed for a fresh start. I just knew there was a better way to live as an adult. As a young adult, not only did I have a lot of boyfriends, but I drank heavily, partied constantly, tried different drugs, could not hold down a job even though, let me tell you, I have had some GREAT ones. I even managed to get an apartment condemned with some friends because we absolutely destroyed the property inside that apartment complex. I would steal to make myself look good. Always thought I had to have the best of things to impress others or take care of others to get them to like me and accept me. How I believed I could do this when I could not hold down a job is completely beyond me. I always tried to not drink, not party, not do drugs and not fall in love with that "Great" guy! I always failed though. I swore this time would be different, but it never was. I would always pray to God and ask him, "why?" "What is wrong with me?" "Why do I keep doing the same crap over and over?" I ALWAYS started out with great.

intentions and something always got in the way, the need to impress others, get them to like me! Little did I know that my troubles accompanied me everywhere I went. I had to fix what was inside of me.

before anything else was fixed. Humph. Who would have thought? What is even worse is once I got these people to like me, I would then keep them at arm's length. Never letting anyone close to me.

Anyway, I learned how to numb all these messed up feelings with one addiction or another. Although I would fight you tooth and nail and tell you, "I'm not addicted!" I covered up every single emotion with anger. When I would start to "feel" I would eat my troubles away, drink the abuse away, drug the nightmares away, and love the loneliness away with a different man. It did not matter who the man was or what kind of man he was if he "LOVED" ME. It did not matter if he abused me or not. The abuse made me feel like, "Oh, he must love me enough to beat me, or else why would he waste his time?" At other times I KNEW I deserved the abuse I was getting dealt. I did not clean the house good enough, or I did not get the laundry done on time, or why did I stare at that man. I must have given him a reason because why else would all these men beat me. It started at the age of 4 and has not stopped yet. I was convinced it was my fault and that I was the one who needed help. That was partly true, I did need help. Help with my low self-esteem, help with my attitude, help with my belief system and help with needing the approval of others.

People do not realize how addictive the need for love can truly be and how much we will do and say just to gain acceptance and love from those who we desire to have in our lives or to keep in our lives. I cannot tell you the things I have done just to gain love and acceptance from some drunk man. I would lie to him to make me appear more interesting or would live a lifestyle that was not what I was truly all about. For all my life I never knew who I really was. Do I like jazz? Do I like a medium rare steak? Do I like to swear? Do I like having pets or no pets? I could not answer these questions because every different man there was a different Nikki. It was a hard life to maintain so it always led to arguments and severe fights because I got tired of living those lies. I do not like waking up to a man who smells like alcohol every morning. It disgusts me but let me tell you I endured it for many years so I would not lose the man who "Loved" me. The list could go on and on.

There are so many addictions that come from not only mental health diseases, but also trauma and abuse that many of us have endured. When a child is abused relentlessly, that tends to color the rest of his life by this trauma. You fail to see reality. You do not know how to reason, or how to figure out what has been done to you is not right. You start to internalize things and you just know that everything is your fault. How can a 4-year-old really control a man or stop him from harming them? They cannot!! It is impossible! Let me tell you though I have spent my entire life convincing myself and others that I could have called the cops, I could have fought these men off, I could have done this or that instead of letting the abuse continue until I was virtually a scared little kid at the age of 41 years old. Hello!!! It WASN'T my fault! What I am responsible for is what I do with the rest of my life here on out.

Hence, why this book is coming into play. I want to open the community's eyes. I want people to realize that the saying 'Guns don't kill people, people kill people! That there is a reason a young man one day seems to be a good solid kid and the next day he goes on a shooting rampage. We need to start opening our eyes to the very real disease that is running rampant in our world today.

I do not have a P.H.D. and I am not some super smart person but what I do have is some very real-life experiences that would break your heart and break many people's spirits. There have been times where I thought I could not take this life anymore, but God had different plans for me, and I believe helping others is that plan.

"WISDOM COMES ALONE THROUGH SUFFERING"

Aeschylus, 525-456 B.C.

CHAPTER TWO

THE STORY OF ADDICTS

We all have goals in life, right? We all want a better life for ourselves, right? So, why not work together to make our world a better place? To love one another and to show kindness instead of hatred? Learn about the different addictions that plague our world.

Addictions have been around for hundreds of years and you would be astounded at the people who have addictions. I am going to share.

some very well-known people who had addictions. Some did not overcome their addictions, and others thank you Jesus had a great support system and were able to pull through those addictions and lead a great inspiring life. Used those addictions that they overcame to bring the WORLD immense joy!   With that said let us look at some of these people!

MILES DEWEY DAVIS THE 3RD

Addictions are found in a wide variety of persons. The community always wants to believe that the lowly people are the ones who suffer from addictions. This is just not true! Miles Dewey Davis was born in 1926 and started to study music in 1939 when he was only 13 years old.

By the age of 16 Miles was a member of the musician's union and working professionally when he was not in school. In 1949 Miles began to use narcotics while playing in Jazz Clubs and which gave Miles the 'IN' with different dealers. By 1950 he had developed a heroin addiction.

Due to this addiction Miles was unreliable and people started to lose trust in him. Including but not limited to his family.

In 1953 when things were completely out of control with Miles he is went back to where his family lived and locked himself in a guest room, for 12 days where he went through severe withdrawal from heroin. He then remained clean and dependable until the fatal day in 1976. Miles had to go.

through some severe medical issues, hip replacement operation, sickle cell disease, depression, bursitis and ulcers. Due to all these issues Miles then renewed his dependence of alcohol and drugs. Once again, Heroin was his drug of choice. Miles ended up dying in 1991 from a stroke, pneumonia and respiratory failure. At the young age of 65 years old!!

Today, people who are addicts know to stay away from pain pills after having surgery, due to this very thing. Heck, most of the time Doctors will not even give narcotics to people who are addicts because they fear it will cause relapse. Because unfortunately once you are addicted to something it is so easy to relapse. All it takes is that one day when you are feeling weak and hopeless.

Elvis Aaron Presley

So now we are going to talk about my favorite person in the world Elvis Aaron Presley. Elvis was born on January 8th, 1935 in Tupelo, Mississippi to Gladys Presley And Vernon Presley. In 1948, Elvis and his parents moved to Memphis, Tennessee where he had attended Humes high school. He began his career there in 1954, with Sun records owner, Sam Phillips, who wanted to   bring the sound of African-American music to a wider audience.

Elvis did much to establish his life. He did so much good. He was so opposed to any recreational drugs, that on December 21, 1970 he paid a visit to President Richard Nixon at the White House after writing a six-page letter requesting this visit asking if he could be a Federal Agent at Large in the Bureau of Narcotics and Drugs. He once told Cassandra Peterson, later known as Elvira that she should never do marijuana again. He was so against any drugs. Elvis was just appalled at her use of Marijuana.

Elvis had a heart of gold! He was not your typical drug addict if there is such a thing as a typical drug addict. He was drafted into the US Army in 1958, where he was then stationed in West Germany and discharged in 1960, as a Sergeant. Elvis had such a heart of gold that in 1975 he purchased an electric wheelchair for a poor black East Memphis woman, and literally picked her up and set her in it. The woman's teenage daughter told Elvis she loved his car. He then gave it to her and even gave her boyfriend a job.

It was then in 19 73 on October 9th, he was now becoming increasingly unwell. Twice during the year, he overdosed on barbiturates, spending three days in a coma in his hotel suite after the first incident. toward the end of 1973, he was hospitalized in a semi-comatose state from the effects of Demerol.

addiction. Elvis claimed that he felt that by getting drugs from a doctor he was not the common everyday junkie getting something off the street. He did not even realize he had a problem, because this doctor was just prescribing away. The doctor ended up losing his license for these actions.

Elvis Presley died at age 42 on August 16th, 1977 at his mansion in Graceland near Memphis, his fans were shocked. Many people believe that he died of a mere heart attack, but this is not the case, his autopsy detected 14 different drugs in his bloodstream, ten of which were in significant quantity.

Not everybody that is an addict is a loser. Elvis did so much with his life. He was ranked number 2 on VH1's 100 Sexiest artist and #8 on VH1's 100 greatest artists of rock and roll he was voted best singer of all time by Q magazine and he was voted the third greatest rock 'n' roll artist of all time by Rolling Stone magazine.

Unfortunately, something significant in somebody's life is usually what leads them to addiction. The hopelessness and the feeling of worthlessness is very overwhelming. When you are at that fork in your life where you do not know which way to turn you do not always make the best decisions.

Billie Holiday

Billie Holiday grew up on the streets of Baltimore as an angry and defiant child. Billy was raped at 10 years old then put in a cell for two days because the police thought she was a prostitute. They finally imprisoned the man for three months for her rape.

At the age of 10, she reported that she had been raped. That claim, combined with her frequent truancy, resulted in her being sent to the House of the Good Shepherd, a Catholic reformed school in 1925. It was only through the assistance of a family friend that she was released two years later. Scared by these experiences, Holiday moved to New York in 1928. In 1929 Holiday's mother discovered a neighbor, Wilbur's rich, in the act of raping her daughter; Rich was sentenced to three months in jail as well.

At 14 years old Billy started to prostitute herself so that she could feed herself. According to Billie holiday's own account, she was recruited by a brothel, worked as a prostitute in 1930, and was eventually imprisoned for a short time for solicitation. In this time Billy started to sing in the nightclubs.

In the early 1940s Billy started to use hard drugs. In 1947 Billy was put into jail on drug charges where she ended up serving eight months at the federal corrections Institute.

Billy tried to quit using heroin many times, even going to the extent of having her friends lock her away in their house while she struggled with the withdrawals and the question of, "Why God, can't I stop?

It is so easy for us to judge other people. If we do not understand what other people are going through, we do tend to judge and wonder why they do the things they do. But once we start hearing people's stories we then realize once again that there is always something that turns them down that Road.

Everybody deals with their issues in different ways. Some people overeat, under eat, smoke, exercise, whatever brings peace of mind to every individual that is what they reach for!

Back in the nineties, anorexia was HUGE! If a man or woman were unhappy with his/her life that started to view themselves as fat and they would turn to making themselves sick. Some people were so addicted to doing this that they ended up dying.

So instead of judging people we need to take the time to get to know people.

I am a HUGE fan of Dhar Mann and his videos. I love the life lessons I am always learning from his videos. There was this one video where this gentleman was walking and there was a homeless man asking for change. The gentleman snapped on the homeless man and told him to stop being lazy and get a job. As he proceeds down the path, he comes across a lady and a young child. The child keeps telling the lady I do not want to eat. The gentleman says, "If you didn't spoil that child like that, she would mind you and eat the sandwich." As the gentleman continues after all his judgements, he comes across a black man who is blind. The black man heard his last interaction and told the gentleman, "Never assume you know people unless you take the time to get to know them." The gentleman pondered on this statement and decided to go back and hear these people's stories. The homeless man was a vet who had no family and no support. He was homeless because he could not find a job when he came home after being deployed. The gentleman was so sorry he apologized and gave him a lot of money. He then went back to the lady and the child. The lady said, "this is my granddaughter, her mom was just killed yesterday and today is very hard on her. The gentleman was beside himself, so he went and bought her a jump rope, and he apologized.

Its things like this that we need to realize. We do not know anyone's story and we should not judge. Every experience is so different.

CHAPTER THREE

THE LIFE OF AN INMATE

I would like to share some very sad yet uplifting stories from people who suffer with some very severe addictions and mental health issues. I want you to see how mental health, trauma and addiction all correlate with one another. I also want you to see the strength it takes to overcome those addictions when you have no one in your life who really gives a damn about you, and how when you do find someone it makes a world of difference. Winnebago mental health offers a reprieve for women and men who suffer from these issues, and they take the time to really treat people's addictions, trauma and abuse and helps people to really learn about themselves. They help them to change their belief system by showing people kindness and allowing them to be themselves. To be able to learn a new way of life. Winnebago mental health and their staff changed my life. I am now a confident woman Who knows the abuse I have endured is not my fault. I have learned I can do anything I put my heart and mind into. No more hearing those voices tell me you are a loser you cannot do this or that. Nope, I know with hard work I can accomplish anything. I never heard that before and neither did a lot of these people. Enjoy their stories, feel their stories. Please open your heart to these women.

Britany

This is the first person I ever sat down to interview for my book. Her story really hit home for me because she struggled and still struggles with gambling. This is a woman who had it all, her husband who would give her the world. Who worked his tail off to provide for his family which included a son who was well loved by both his parents? Looking in from the outside you would believe this family had it all. No problems no aggravations the perfect family.

Then Britney's whole world started to spin in the wrong direction. Something in her mind just snapped. She believed people were trying to poison her family's food. She became very paranoid in her own home. Britney suffers from some severe mental health issues such as bipolar and paranoia and PTSD and these became apparent in her actions but no one, including Brittany realized what was going on.

Then one thing led to another. Britany's paranoia started making Britney leaving her house in the frigid cold because her fear was so pronounced. Then this led to her gambling. Her gambling became so severe not only was she lying about what she was doing, but how she was getting the money. Which she was getting the money by embezzling money from each of her different jobs. Why was she embezzling this money you may ask? To support her addiction and pay bills because she lost so much of the money her and her husband made. In order to hide her addiction and the loss of money the only out she could see was to embezzle from her jobs.

Britney has been in prison twice for a total of Seven years and eight months and has now only realized the severity of her mental health issues. She is currently receiving help finally for the mental health issues, but it is very hard work. Every day is a struggle for her, but she believes that if she continues her medications, she will be OK. It is not easy when you start to change yourself. First you must take a good hard look at who you are and then who you want to be. You must learn how to stop lying to yourself and to realize that you do have a problem. Many of us do not like to do that it is so much easier to just point fingers at everybody else then to admit that we have a problem. The one thing with Britney is she is 55 years old; she has felonies for embezzling, struggles with her mental health disease. So how will she get a job? How will she ever be able to afford to get help to pay for her medications she is also alone now. Her husband divorced her, and her son will not have anything to do with her period she has been imprisoned with no outside support. So, when she gets out, she will have to rely on herself. How many of us can walk through life completely alone? It is not impossible but it sure is a lonely existence and unfortunately it could lead Brittany down the path of destruction and despair.

This is what I want to avoid for people. I want to help people in the community to see the issues at hand and work together to help make the community/ world a better place. Not just for us but for all future generations. You will see many people stories that will break your heart, make you angry maybe even disgust you but I would really like to take a stand and make a difference. Currently compassion and kindness is one of the biggest things that this world is lacking also understanding. So, let us start to understand how trauma, mental health issues and addictions all correlate as one.

Chaka

Chaka is a young minded 24-year-old. I do not mean young minded as in not intelligence. I mean young minded as in she has been incarcerated since she was 18 years old and has not had a real chance to experience life as an adult. She has basically grown up in the prison system. Chaka has had a very sad life. Her biological mother was a severe drug addict and alcoholic. There was molestation from one family member to the next. Her whole biological family has suffered from one trauma and abuse to the next, as well as one addiction to the next.

Chaka was adopted by a wonderful family. Now here is the great part that I really want to point out especially with everything going on in the world today. Chaka is a young black woman who was adopted by an all-white family. Her adopted family has stuck by her during her entire incarceration and will continue to do so once she is released which will be very soon. The reason Chaka is in prison, is because she had been brutally raped and in retaliation, she attempted to burn down the offender's house. She did not commit this crime alone or even think about doing this crime alone. Her very angry boyfriend presented the idea to Chaka and in her angry, hurt, shameful, embarrassed and young mind thought it was a great way to get back at her offender. Unfortunately, I know this man who did this to Chaka. I know how he has laughed about how he got away with his raping of Chaka, but Chaka has had to grow up in prison.

Chaka has suffered some very serious traumas in her life, so her self-esteem is very low. Her addiction in life is to be attracted to the very unhealthy relationships that lead to physical, mental, and sexual abuse. It does not matter if it is by man or woman women. All Chaka wants in life is to be accepted for who she is and to be loved. Her biggest fear is being abandoned it happened to her once why would not happen again?

Chaka has paid for her crime, but she will always have to live with what has been done to her and what she has done to others. As an innocent child. Chaka suffers from mental health disease as well. She has been diagnosed with manic depression and social anxiety disorder. Chaka has some serious fears about getting released. By the time I write this book she will have already been released for three years. Shaq's biggest struggle is her ability to feel accepted by herself and others. After growing up in prison you start to doubt any self-worth you may have had at one time period and how much self-worth does an 18-year-old feel? Chaka has issues dealing with abandonment. Growing up she has experienced so many people leaving her or abusing her that now she does not know who to trust and believe that they will not have abandoned her once again.

She has many issues surrounding her own self birth, feeling unwanted, unloved and not fitting in. Because of these issues she tends to push people away when they start to get close to her period, I know this is a fact because it was done to me by her.

But I let her know I would not leave her side. Two things that Chaka longs for the most in her future is to obtain a degree in veterinarian, get married and most definitely have a healthy child. Just to be successful in her own life. Chaka has many more dreams and goals in her life will she accomplish them only Chaka knows. The other big question is, will the community accept her as a different person or treat her like the young delusional child she once was?

Danielle

Danielle is someone who has dealt with addiction most of her life. Not just within herself, but also with her mother and father. Her mother died from a heroin overdose and her father who acquired hepatitis C died from severe alcohol disease. This is the only life that Danielle knew. She ended up getting into heroin and cocaine as well. Danielle has been cleaned by being forced into prison, like so many addicts have period unfortunately you do not learn a whole lot about clean living when you are forced into it. And, when you go to prison it is truly easier to get drugs inside the prison system than it is on the streets. Danielle did go into a treatment facility which has helped her with some of her inner demons which are the biggest reasons most people turn to an addiction of one type or another period many people get out of prison and go back to what they know, who they are comfortable with. If we can help ourselves and one another deal with the traumas we have endured, we have a better chance at stopping the recidivism rate.

. Danielle's biggest fear is relapsing because she knows that if she goes down that Road again there will not be any coming back for her. She will end up dead and that is not what she wants for her future and she most definitely does not want to put her family through that again. Especially after all the loss they have had to endure already. Some things that Danielle wants for her future is to find simplicity in everyday living period to remain drug free and just to have the coping skills to deal with everyday stressors period to have the capability to have a family and just be happy and at peace.

Amanda

This is a woman I hold near and dear even though she does not know it, because of her situation. She is 35 years old and looking at 30 more years in prison period she committed burglary to support her cocaine habit. Her parents realized that she had an addiction to cocaine and kicked her out after trying outpatient on steam once a week. They felt like she was not worth anymore time or money. She also has two brothers who were out doing their own thing and did not realize the depth of her addiction.

Amanda has been to prison 3 times and all of them were for burglary to support her cocaine habit.

This seems to be the way we (the community and the justice system) deal with addiction. Let us just throw them in prison and hope they get rehabilitated when it is so much easier to get drugs while being in prison. Amanda struggles with being accepted by herself and from others. To endure this pain that she has, she tends to self-harm which is just another form of addiction. A way of releasing the pain that you feel deep down in your soul, knowing in your heart that you are not worthy of anyone's acceptance, or love. I mean how do you know how to accept yourself when others never have?

Amanda really fears never being able to be part of her parents lives and them dying before she even gets out of prison period on the other hand, she does hold out hope that one day she can be a part of her family's life whether she is in prison or out. She just wants them to see her love her be there with her. She would also like to become a journalist/ novelist one day. She loves to read and to write. She is very curious about life and the future. She is so intelligent, and I do not use that word loosely she could have such a great future if she can just get out with not just her addiction but also her mental health issues. A few things that Amanda suffers from his PTS D, antisocial personality disorder and personality disorder and drug dependency. You do not get in depth help with addictions while in prison. There are many statistics that show that the programs that are being offered in prisons today are so outdated. They are like from the 90's and have been proven that the way they do things do not work. Like the AODA program!!

Debbie

Debbie is a 55-year-old woman who has been incarcerated two times in the state prison. One is real life prison and the other is the prison within herself. Debbie suffers from Major Depressive Disorder, Borderline Personality Disorder, Suicidal Tendency, and alcoholism. She even once suffered from Postpartum Blues.

Debbie has had some sporadic support from her children and some by her Sister and Brother. Otherwise, she has been doing time by herself. She is incarcerated for killing her husband who was severely abusive. She was charged for first degree intentional homicide which here was several addictions in Debbie's life when she committed this crime. Debbie was addicted to alcohol and marijuana.

Debbie's husband was very abusive in a physical, mental and sexual manner and she was not allowed to share the abuse with anyone. It was all hush hush. Boy, do I understand this. The fear of telling anyone yet the NEED to tell someone. When she would try to share these issues with her mother, father and siblings it was almost like SHE was doing something wrong.

One of the biggest obstacles that Debbie faces is being able to accept people for who they are. Not having the opportunity nor the power to change people or getting others to WANT to change.

Now, I share these few stories to show you this. Every single one of these women have had some severe things happen to them. Things that would break a lesser man or woman. Things that would cause others to commit suicide.   I am not making excuses for these women, just trying to get people to try to understand what leads some people down that wrong path.

CHAPTER FOUR

<u>ADDICTIONS AND WHAT THEY REPRESENT</u>

I would like to share with you the different addictions and how substance abuse, childhood trauma and mental health issues all correlate with one another. I would like to take this time to expose the traumatic experiences especially those occurring in young children. What a lot of people do not realize is that children who struggle with abuse are more than likely going to experience Post-Traumatic Stress Disorder. As young children, we have no idea that what is being done to us is wrong. That this abuse is not acceptable. We then learn habits and strategies to protect ourselves from the potential abuse that comes from getting to know others. A big one is manipulating and hurting others before they can hurt us. Making someone else's life so miserable because we are so miserable within ourselves. We do not know that we are miserable, or unhappy because we've never genuinely experienced happiness. We just think that this misery we feel is part of everyday life.

For all my 40 years of life anger was my first and only emotion. Now I am 43 years old and just now learning that there are so many levels of emotions and it is okay to feel all of them.

I am learning how to identify certain emotions and let me tell you it is very frustrating to be as old as I am and have no clue what I am feeling at a certain time. I must sit there and talk myself through it all just to find out what I am feeling. I still resort to anger quite often. I just realized not too long ago that when I am afraid, I get super angry and lash out. Is this really anger? No! It is fear! You may ask yourself, why is she making such a big deal out of this feeling stuff, well, let me tell you, it is a big deal! Because everything we do and accomplish is based on feeling.

Now, the unfortunate part is because I had no one to turn to I turned to alcohol, drugs and men. None of which was good for me. I tried to please men at whatever cost, and it usually just got me beat, raped, yelled at and belittled. Always ending in me feeling like I was a nothing. Drugs got me into trouble as did alcohol. My stress level would be so high just having people around me and I would act out in anger and not even understand why I was so angry. Little did I know that I also struggled with PTSD, Bi-Polar, Personality Disorder, Manic depression disorder and Social Anxiety Disorder.

I did not know I had these mental health issues at the time. I was diagnosed with them after I got involved in a horrific crime. Which I will share with you later in this book. Not knowing I had these disorders led me down a very bad path. I never understood what was wrong inside my brain. Heck, I did not know that the life I was leading was any different from anyone else, because of the people I surrounded myself with. They were the same.

Many people I came to find out had these same "disorders" and suffered with different addictions to either numb the pain they were feeling, stop the voices that were in their heads, or just to be able to get out of bed, and live life.

Now the addictions I am going to speak on are all factual and true. None of it is based on experience only research. I did not want to put MY experiences in this part, only the researched so it is not called "Bias." The first addiction is: PROBLEM GAMBLING

Problem Gambling is associated with increased suicidal ideation and attempts compared to the general population. Between 12% and 24% pathological gamblers attempt suicide. Other factors that increase the risk in problem gamblers include mental illness, alcohol, and drug misuse.

Low levels of brain-derived neurotrophic factor (BDNF) are both directly associated with suicide and indirectly associated through its role in major depression, PTSD, schizophrenia, obsessive-compulsive disorder, border line personality disorder and finally multiple personality disorder.

Postmortem studies have found reduced levels of BDNF in the hippos' campus and prefrontal cortex, in those with and without psychiatric conditions. Serotonin, a brain neurotransmitter, is believed to be low in those who commit suicide. This is partly based on evidence of increased levels of 5-HT2A receptors found after death. Other evidence includes reduced levels of a breakdown product of serotonin, 5-hydroxyindoleacetic acid, in the cerebral spinal fluid. Direct evidence is however hard to gather.

(Epigenetics, the study of changes in genetic expression in response to environmental factors which do not alter the underlying DNA, is also believed to play a role in determining suicide risk.)

CHAPTER FIVE

STATISTICS OF ADDICTIONS AND INCARCERATION

This chapter is very hard for me to speak on because I lost a loved one due to this addiction. I was unable to help this loved one and it is one of my biggest regrets and disappointments. The reason I was not able to help this loved one is because for one I was in prison for being party to a crime. A crime that took me away from family and friends for ten long years. I had absolutely no control. The second reason is, I had no understanding of what this addiction was truly like. I did not know the facts nor the severity of this addiction.

I still did not even after her death until I started doing research on this book and realizing my own addictions. The guilt and disgust that I feel to this day is horrific. The guilt for being so selfish and ending up in prison when she needed me the most is so profound and that is the main reason for this book. I wanted to learn all that I could about drugs, addictions, and the signs. I also wanted to help others know these things as well so they never have to feel the way I feel or lose someone without doing everything they can to help that other person.

What I am going to share with you are the statistics of opioid addiction. It may just surprise you how high these statistics are. You will see how more than half of state prisoners and two-thirds of sentenced jail inmates met the criteria for drug dependence or abuse according to data collected through the National Inmate Surveys (NIS). There are also many who have died in prison, jail or after being released from a facility that do not apply to these statistics. The following chart will show you the admission trend for drug offenses.

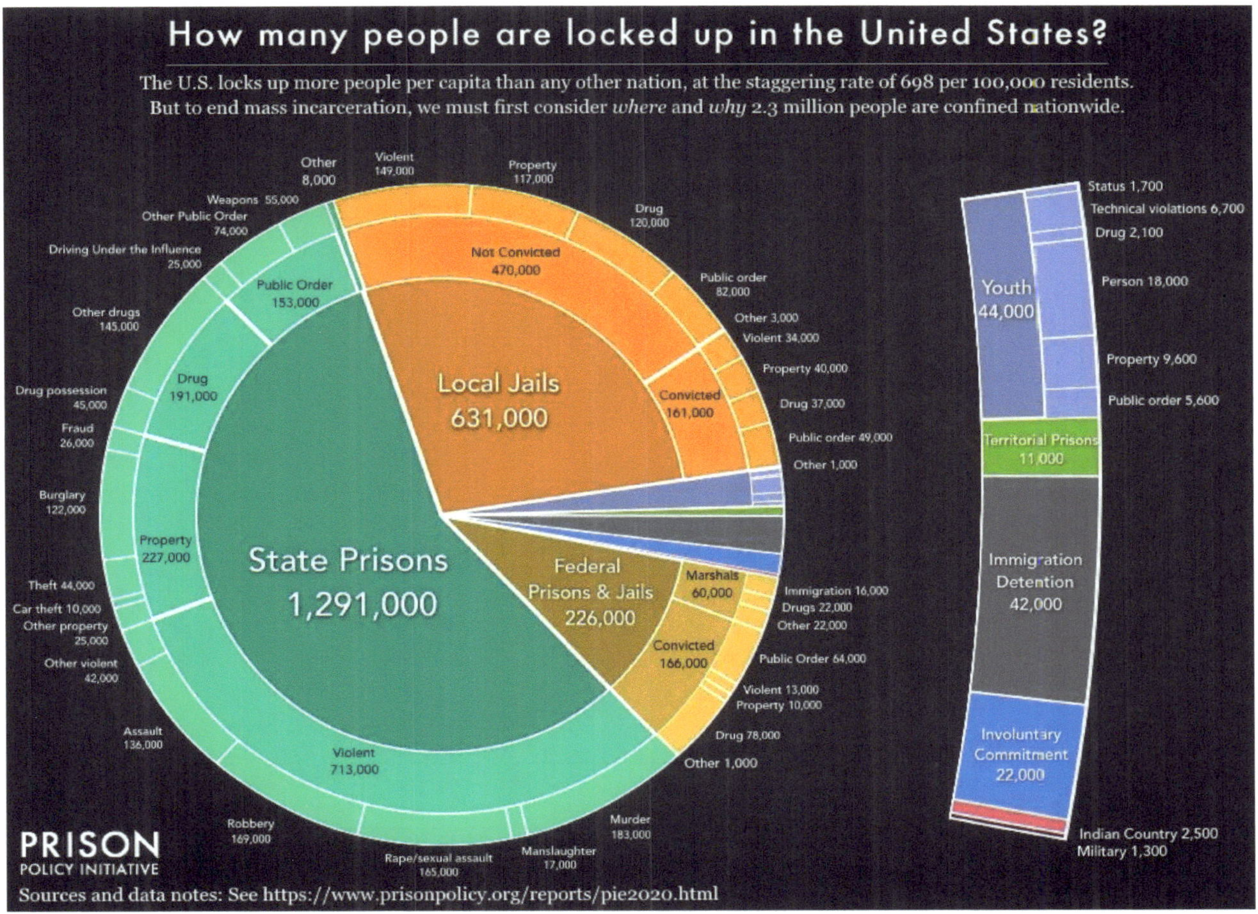

How many people are locked up in the United States?
The U.S. locks up more people per capita than any other nation, at the staggering rate of 698 per 100,000 residents.
But to end mass incarceration, we must first consider where and why 2.3 million people are confined nationwide.
Other 8,000
Violent 149,000
Property 117,000
Weapons 55,000
Other Public Order 74,000
Driving Under the Influence 25,000
Drug 120,000
Public Order 153,000
Not Convicted 470,000
Public order 82,000
Other drugs 145,000
Other 3,000
Violent 34,000
Drug possession 45,000
Drug 191,000
Local Jails 631,000
Property 40,000
Convicted 161,000
Fraud 26,000
Drug 37,000
Burglary 122,000
Public order 49,000
Other 1,000
Property 227,000
Theft 44,000
State Prisons 1,291,000
Federal Prisons & Jails 226,000
Marshals 60,000
Immigration 16,000
Car theft 10,000
Other property 25,000
Drugs 22,000
Other 22,000
Other violent 42,000
Convicted 166,000
Public Order 64,000
Assault 136,000
Violent 713,000
Violent 13,000
Property 10,000
Drug 78,000
Other 1,000
Robbery 169,000
Murder 183,000
Rape/sexual assault 165,000
Manslaughter 17,000
Status 1,700
Technical violations 6,700
Drug 2,100
Youth 44,000
Person 18,000
Property 9,600
Public order 5,600
Territorial Prisons 11,000
Immigration Detention 42,000
Involuntary Commitment 22,000
Indian Country 2,500
Military 1,300
PRISON POLICY INITIATIVE
Sources and data notes: See https://www.prisonpolicy.org/reports/pie2020.html

Now this is the chart of how many people are incarcerated for all kinds of things. But let us look further into this. I found this fact in the (NIS) it appalled me!

"true that police, prosecutors, and judges continue to punish people harshly for nothing more than drug possession. Drug offenses still account for the incarceration of almost half a million people."

When they say drug offenses, they do not tell you WHAT the drug offenses are. People who are high commit crimes so they can get more drugs. Rob people, harm people, things they would never do sober, but the addiction is so pronounced they do stuff to feed the demon.

This is just part of the research I have found. Now I am going to get to the nitty gritty of the subject. Show you stuff I have found through NIS and it is devastating to see how full the prisons and jails are with drug related charges.

PRISON ADMISSION TRENDS BY DRUG OFFENSE TYPE (2000-2016)

Office of the Secretary Research and Policy Unit

ADMISSION YEAR	TOTAL PRISON ADMISSIONS	ANY DRUG OFFENSE	% OF TOTAL ADMISSIONS
2008	9947	2642	26.60%
2009	9445	2390	25.30%
2010	8980	2361	26.30%
2011	8427	1980	23.50%
2012	8172	1937	23.70%
2013	8701	2116	24.30%
2014	8862	2291	25.90%
2015	8840	2303	26.10%
2016	9116	2448	26.90%

ADMISSIONS WITH ANY DRUG OFFENSE

PERCENT BY RISK TO REOFFEND

PERCENT OF PRISON POPULATION WITH A SUBSTANCE ABUSE NEED 69.0%

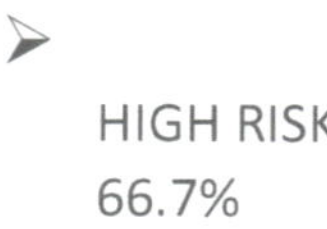

HIGH RISK
66.7%

> MEDIUM RISK
> 25.8%

> LOW RISK
> 7.5%

WHITE OFFENDERS		BLACK OFFENDERS	
OPIOID	13.8%	OPIOID	7.40%
COCAINE	3.6%	COCAINE	12.1%
THC	5.9%	THC	7.1%
AMEHETAMINE	6.6%	AMEHETAMINE	0.5%

In 2016, prison admissions for cocaine and THC offenses were higher for black offenders. In contrast, opioid and amphetamine offenses were higher for white offenders.

We know that the use of alcohol and drugs can negatively affect all aspects of a person's life. Do you believe that sentencing a drug addict to ten years in prison is going to help his/her addiction? Let me tell you, my ex was once in prison and he said, "Nikki, getting drugs in prison is so much easier then when you're on the streets." I did not believe him. Coming to prison has completely changed my attitude.   I was naïve, but after being in prison for ten years and seeing the determination of the inmates and their friends or family that helped them, I can tell you that the statement my ex made is very true! I had never seen heroin before until I was IN prison. I saw pills that I did not know existed. I literally got a full college education in knowing what drugs look like, taste like, feel like, how much they cost, and the list goes on and on. No, I did not do the drugs I just paid very close attention to my surroundings. You never knew when someone would plant the drugs on you or in your cell. So, if you were not observant you could become an innocent victim. It scares me how graphic these addicts can be, almost like you can feel, or taste what they felt or tasted. If I so chose to become a drug dealer in my future life, I now know the ins and outs of it. My point in all this, is sending addicts to prison is not helping them or the community, it is most definitely hindering them. The reason I say it is hindering them is because they do not have all the tools, they need so they guess how much they should take which was a direct result of overdosing. I cannot even tell you how many people died in the ten years I was there as a direct result of overdosing. How many almost died. It is truly sad!

 If you can go into the prison system not knowing a thing about drugs and then ten years later come out having a full education, just think how hard it must be for an addict who so desperately wants to get clean. Life is very hard on any addict.

Addiction is a compulsive physiological need for and use of a habit-forming substance (heroin, nicotine, or alcohol) characterized by tolerance and by well-defined physiological symptoms upon withdrawal. Would you put a nicotine addict in prison? Or would you try to find help for him/her to get the help they need? People do not look at how nicotine effects people's lives. This is a subject I can relate to very well. I used to smoke 2 packs of cigarettes a day. Lord forgive me, but when I would run out of cigarettes it would warrant very homicidal tendencies in me. I would be so angry and would treat people like they had offended me or did something horrific to me. I would start fights with whomever met me just because I needed that cigarette so badly. Then once I took that deep inhale of smoke it was like everything in the world was ok again! I look back at how my addiction would make me react. I would go and steal from Wal-Mart just so I could return things and get the cash so I could go and buy cigarettes. Addiction is horrific. It is demeaning and embarrassing! It makes you do things you never thought you would do in your life.

There was this mother of three who was in prison with me. She was my cell mate. She was crying one day, and I asked her if she was ok. She said I need help. I am in here for robbing a pharmacy with my husband. I lost everything for that hit, and I still desire and need that high. She said to me with tears in her eyes, "what kind of mother does this?" She was just a child herself. An addict. It broke my heart. While she was beating herself up, she still craved that high. Needed that high. Whole time regretting what she had caused not only to her children but to the community.

I had it easy. My addictions were so much less yet so hard then what others face. I can only imagine how awful other addictions must be. Drugs attack the mind, the nervous system, make you do things that you would NEVER do while sober.

I have heard so many stories since I have been incarcerated that it just breaks my heart. The suicidal tendencies, the needle marks on people's arms, legs even between their toes, groin, breast, and neck. Unless you are mainlining then you go in the aortic artery. It gets to your system a lot faster. This way has killed so many people. Do you really believe a high- school student, who is getting straight A's, has a football scholarship, friends, family, a future, really wants to turn into a drug addict? Wants to end their life by shooting up in their aortic artery. No! This is not the life they would choose. Someone says, "Dude you've got to try this, it will help you stay awake longer, practice harder, feel better about yourself." You think, oh one time will not do nothing! Unfortunately, that one time is all it takes. Now that football star with a scholarship is shooting up, laying in the street, literally dying because their body is going through withdrawals. They then go rob someone so they can get that next hit, so they are not feeling like death and the cycle goes on.

Come on, People, we need to start having compassion. Stop judging! Start becoming aware of what these people are enduring. Yes! They are victims. Yes! They do struggle. Yes! They are killing themselves.

How can we help them instead of incarcerating them? You ever wonder why people commit suicide as addicts?

Suicide is often committed out of despair, the cause of which is frequently attributed to a mental disorder such as depression, bipolar disorder, schizophrenia, or drug abuse. Factors that affect the risk of suicide include psychiatric disorders, drug misuse, psychological states, cultural, family, and social situations, and genetics. Mental illness and substance misuse frequently co-exist. Other risk factors include having previously attempted suicide, the ready availability of a means to commit the act a family history of suicide, or the presence of traumatic brain injury. Mental disorders are often present at the time of suicide with estimates ranging from 27% to more than 90%.

Of those who have been admitted to a psychiatric unit their lifetime risk of completed suicide is about 8.6%. Half of all people who die by suicide may have major depressive disorder; having this or one of the other mood disorders such as bipolar disorder increases the use of drugs.   A poor ability to solve problems the loss of abilities one used to have, and poor impulse control also play a role. In older adults the perception of being a burden to others causes them to turn to drugs as well.

The Justice System believes in forcing addicts to abstain by placing them in jail/prison. Little do they realize that first, forcing someone to withdrawal can literally kill someone. Then they are not learning new skills, they are just temporarily abstaining then go out into the streets where they get drunk and get high and then people overdose because they do not realize that they are using too much because they are using what they have always used. Hence why not only educating the community but everyone on the seriousness of addiction.

The prison systems in the State of Wisconsin are not only using outdated material but it has shown that 73% of the people that have gone through the AODA programs have relapsed.

1 out of 100 people will achieve long term sobriety, so why isn't the Justice System helping these people with the serious help they need? Why wouldn't we invest some money into real programs that could potentially save so many lives? Why are people covering up the truth to the community about the real life struggles that addicts face? At the end of the day, it is all about money. Listen, as taxpayers, YOU are paying for these addicts to continually come back to prison. They are not getting the help they need. They are not learning anything. They have no coping skills. No support system. They KNOW prison. It is the playground for drugs. The state gets paid $50,000 a year per inmate. Which estimates to be about $43 billion just for state prisons. That does NOT include the medical care that is provided. Which is about $8.1 billion. All YOUR money as a taxpayer! Hard working residents of the community. Wouldn't it make more sense to get them freedom from drugs, so you can have freedom in your wallet? It is time to look behind the scenes. I realize it can be scary, maybe even heart wrenching, but we need to stop acting like the ostrich and burying our heads in the sand and face the truth!!!

 bury/hide one's head in the sand, to
To ignore danger, unpleasantness, or the like by pretending not to see it. The term comes from the practice of ostriches, who spend a good deal of time burrowing headfirst in the sand. Most of the time they are eating, for these large, flightless birds consume sand and gravel, which are used in their gizzards to help digest food. However, it was long thought that they put their heads down in the mistaken belief that they then cannot be seen, and from the early seventeenth century on this mythical self-delusion was transferred to human beings who are avoiding unpleasantness.

CHAPTER SIX

THE ADDICTION OF METHAMPHETAMINES

How many of you know what methamphetamine is? Do not worry a lot of people do not know what it is or what it does. It seems like as soon as we get a handle on a certain drug and the effects it has; the drug users have found something different to try.

Let me share with you a very powerful, addictive stimulant that dramatically affects the central nervous system. This drug is made easily in clandestine laboratories with relatively inexpensive over the counter ingredients.

This drug has the potential to become the most widespread drug abuse known to our world. This drug has been around for a very long time. Methamphetamine is commonly known as meth, speed, and chalk. In its smoked form, it is often referred to as ice, crystal, crank, and glass. It is a white odorless, butter tasting crystalline powder that dissolves in water or alcohol. This drug was developed early in this century from its parent drug, amphetamine and was used originally in nasal decongestants and bronchial inhalers.

Methamphetamine's cause an increase in activity, a decrease in appetite, and just a general sense of being right with the world or just having a sense of well-being. According to the 2000 National Household Survey on Drug Abuse, an estimated 8.8 million people have tried methamphetamine at one point in their lives. This is a worldwide addiction. Hawaii and other major western cities such as San Francisco, Denver, and Los Angeles seem to suffer more. It is very accessible to get this is causing a rise in concern. The drug abuse treatment admissions reported by the Community Epidemiology Work Group (CEWG) showed in 2001 that methamphetamine remained the leading drug of abuse among treatment clients.

Methamphetamine can be used in a variety of ways. It can be smoked, snorted, orally ingested, or injected. The drug alters the mood in different ways depending on how the drug is used. Immediately after smoking the drug or injecting it intravenously, the user experiences an intense rush or "flash" that lasts only a few minutes and is described as extremely pleasurable.

Snorting or oral ingestion produces euphoria- a high but not an intense rush. Snorting produces effects within three to four minutes and oral ingestion produces effects within fifteen to eighteen minutes.

SHORT-TERM EFFECTS MAY INCLUDE BUT ARE NOT LIMITED TO:

- Increased attention and decreased fatigue
- Increased activity
- Decreased appetite
- Euphoria and rush
- Increased respiration
- Hypothermia

LONG-TERM EFFECTS MAY INCLUDE BUT ARE NOT LIMITED TO:

- Paranoia
- Hallucinations
- Mood disturbances
- Repetitive motor activity
- Stroke
- Weight loss

Now I am going to talk about a very serious consequence for being a methamphetamine abuser. Did you know that people are more at risk for contracting HIV/AIDS and Hepatitis B&C? This is also riskier if you inject this.

Infection with HIV and other infectious diseases are spread among injection users because people get so high and so desperate that they begin to share needles. One person said to me that she did not even know that she was using a broken needle! This is a very risky situation. I am not saying that all drugs are not risky, just that some are riskier in a different way.

The most common treatment that they find works the best is cognitive behavioral intervention. These approaches are designed to help modify the patient's thinking, expectancy, and behaviors, and give them different coping skills.

Here is the problem. You have two parents who find their son/daughter high as a kite in their basement. What do they do? They give their son/ daughter ultimatum. The son/daughter makes all kinds of promises that they will quit. Promises that they truly intend to keep. A couple of days later the parents find their child doing the same thing in their garage. Now what do they do? They kick their kid out of the house because they have no understanding whatsoever of what someone realizes they cannot just stop on their own. Therefore, I want to educate people so maybe we can save some lives here. Did you learn anything from reading my book? Can you feel the pain that some of these people are going through? I hope so, because if you cannot then I sure wasted a whole lot of time writing this book.

"Nothing is so painful to the human mind as a great and sudden change."

Mary Wollstonecraft Shelley

1797-1851

CHAPTER SEVEN

THE COURAGE TO MAKE A DIFFERENCE

How many times have you said to yourself, hmm…I am not going to get involved in that situation because it is not my business? I know I probably did this daily. How many times have you said, well, I will get involved when he/she asks me for help or my advice? Let me tell you, my friend that sometimes people will never verbally ask you for help. Whether it be pride, fear or being raised that asking for help is a sign of weakness. My biggest thing to this day, is if you ask someone for help, they will use it against you or make you pay some price that is not within the norm. Beating you up, raping you, whatever they feel the help is worth. I have a very kind Christian friend who has been such a huge help and I always tell her I feel so bad accepting your help. For the first time EVER in my life, I have heard the words, do not feel bad and most importantly she has never thrown it in my face. We need to have enough compassion within ourselves, to observe what is going on in someone's life. Are they acting out of their norm? Are they acting more aggressively? More isolated? Are they crying> Are they continuously missing work or school when they never used to miss a day? Now, let us be honest, we all have bad days, right? But not every single day. Now if a person is normally negative suddenly life is a bowl of cherries and rainbows, I would advise you to check in with them.

Its ok to show someone some compassion and let them know if they want to talk, you are there for them. I remember a time in my life when I was so fed up with life. I had stage three cancer, had to leave my home, due to my landlord not renewing my lease, lost my best-friend, relationship was going down the drains, and I was just exhausted. Tired of fighting. I wrote notes to everyone that I loved, put all my belongings on Facebook to give a way. Never said a word to anyone about my plan to commit suicide. Then later that day, my good friend Tamra, reached out to me and she said, "what's going on, Nikki?" I told her nothing was wrong, life was good. She probed a little bit deeper, and I just broke down. Shared everything that was going on in my life and she told me to take a minute to breathe. Focus on this second instead of focusing on all the bad that was going on and trying to figure out how I was going to fix things. Her compassion that day literally saved my life and gave me a new perspective on life.

In Brene' Brown's book DARING GREATLY she talks about common humanity. What do you consider common humanity? Well for myself it is when you recognize the feeling of others, listen to someone you normally would not give a second glance to. Smiling at your enemy, reaching out to a stranger who is sitting on a park bench crying or who just seems sad. Doing things, you would want someone else to do for you. Let us take the time to show some compassion to those who have struggles with addiction, trauma, abuse or anyone that seems different from us. Now that is courage.

You do not know how many battles someone has fought, and is still standing, or how many have cried a thousand tears and are still smiling, has been broken, betrayed, abandoned, lost people, and been rejected and are still walking around. These are the people that can humble us, bring us to our knees with their stories, their experiences!! So please have the courage to look beyond the cover of the book and take the time to hear what their story is all about. You never know whose life you could be saving just by saying "Good Morning & Have a nice day!" Or in the end who may change your life!!

I put this little part in because as I continue in this book there will be things that will astound you, possibly break your heart a little bit. I want there to be awareness in how people are and what a little compassion can do! Just like Tamra did for me…..Save a life!!!!

This is what courage is truly all about!!!

"Courage is doing what you're afraid to do. There can be no courage unless you're scared."

Edward Vernon Rickenbacker 1890-1973

CHAPTER EIGHT

COMPASSION AND WHAT IT CAN TRULY ACCOMPLISH

This is a subject that I was not sure I was going to put in this book because it is a very hard subject in so many ways. When I looked up compassion in the Oxford dictionary it gave this definition.

†**1.** Suffering together with another, participation in suffering; fellow-feeling, sympathy.

    a. The feeling or emotion, when a person is moved by the suffering or distress of another, and by the desire to relieve it; pity that inclines one to spare or to succor.

    b. *to have compassion*: to have pity, take pity. So †*to take compassion (upon, of)*

I then went to the Strong's Exhaustive Concordance of the Bible and its definition for the word compassion is this: to be moved as to one's bowels, hence, to be moved with compassion, have compassion (for the bowels were thought to be the seat of love and pity) Pretty close in definition, right? Sounds easy to do right?

Do you ever drive by a homeless person and try to avoid eye contact? Thinking if you do not look at them, pretend not to see them, that it will not hurt them? They will not notice you just driving by them. Or do you say, Wow! Thank God I am not that person? Or worse yet does that homeless person ask you for a dollar or some measly change and you tell him/her no when you know darn well you have three quarters in your pocket?

It is hard for us as a community to understand 'why' people are homeless or to even reach out a compassionate hand because we believe that people deserve what they get. One day I was driving home from the casino and I had won quite a bit of money. I was just coming off the highway when I saw a bearded man on the side of the street holding up a sign which said, I am homeless and very hungry, could you please donate some money so that I can eat? I was so angry. I said to the guy I was with at the time, "yeah right! He is hungry, he does not look hungry to me, all he will do is go buy some booze or drugs. Why would anyone help him? That was the old Nikki!

Probably 20 years later, I was driving to my boyfriend's main office and saw a homeless man. I pulled over and talked to him for a bit of time. He had just come home from the military. Had no family, no friends and no support. He was waiting on disability and could only get so much help.   went home and made him some homemade spaghetti and cookies. Brought them back and gave him some money as well. My heart hurt for this man who had fought for our country only to be treated like this!! Where is the compassion in our world? How did we become so selfish and self-centered?

Yes, many people would go and buy booze with that money. How sad is that to have an addiction so strong and debilitating that you would literally take your last dollar and go spend it on alcohol or drugs?

Do you think these people really want to live like this? No!! Trust me they do not!!   What does God tell us in Hebrews 13:2? *"Be not forgetful to entertain strangers: for thereby some have entertained angels unawares."*

Yikes, can you imagine that maybe that guy that I passed up could have been an angel waiting for me? Someone that could have changed my life in so many ways. Or maybe I could have changed theirs with that little bit of compassion? How sad!

That happened so long ago, yet it still haunts me. Many times, I wonder what happened to that man. What if I could have changed the course of that person's life by my compassion? What if that person could have changed the course of my life? I cannot go back to that day, but I sure can live my life with compassion every day to the fullest!!

How can we say we love others yet drive right by them? Or even our own family who is struggling with addiction and we turn our backs on them and claim it is all out of "tough love." That is crap! We are turning our back because we either lack compassion or we just do not understand what they are going through!

I used to be that person! Judgmental, rude, inconsiderate and selfish. Had no understanding of what people's lives really looked like. Always judging the book by its cover. Many addicts are searching for someone to understand their pain. Show them compassion. Give them the support they so desperately need. And yes, grabbing them and giving them a hug and asking, "what can I do to help?" Have you ever needed a day off from work because your child is sick? You call your boss and explain the situation to him, right? This could go two ways. One your boss could lack all compassion and say to you, "look I really don't care if your child is sick, I need you here. Find someone to take care of him/her and get to work. Now you have never missed work, you do not come in late, you work a lot of overtime and you go beyond your job duties. You feel like you are not expecting much, right? Well, how is this situation any different than that military man who served his country? It is not!!

In 1Peter 3:8-14

[8] Finally, be ye all of one mind, having compassion one of another, love as brethren, be pitiful, be courteous:

[9] Not rendering evil for evil or railing for railing: but contrariwise blessing; knowing that ye are thereunto called, that ye should inherit a blessing.

[10] For he that will love life, and see good days, let him refrain his tongue from evil, and his lips that they speak no guile:

[11] Let him eschew evil, and do good; let him seek peace, and ensue it.

[12] For the eyes of the Lord are over the righteous, and his ears are open unto their prayers: but the face of the Lord is against them that do evil.

[13] And who is her that will harm you, if ye be followers of that which is good?

[14] But and if ye suffer for righteousness' sake, happy are ye: and be not afraid of their terror, neither be troubled.

I really struggle with this one myself daily, sometimes even on a second-to-second basis. If I hear someone that is swearing nonstop, I am like holy cats what is wrong with him? How ignorant!! Am I showing compassion? NO! I am totally judging that person instead of asking if he is ok. I believe therefore there are so many people in prison today, no one wants to take time out of their busy schedule to help someone else in their time of need.

We really need to start treating others the way we want to be treated. If we all reach out to ONE person imagine the possibilities. The world could be a much better place. Mahatma Gandhi once said,

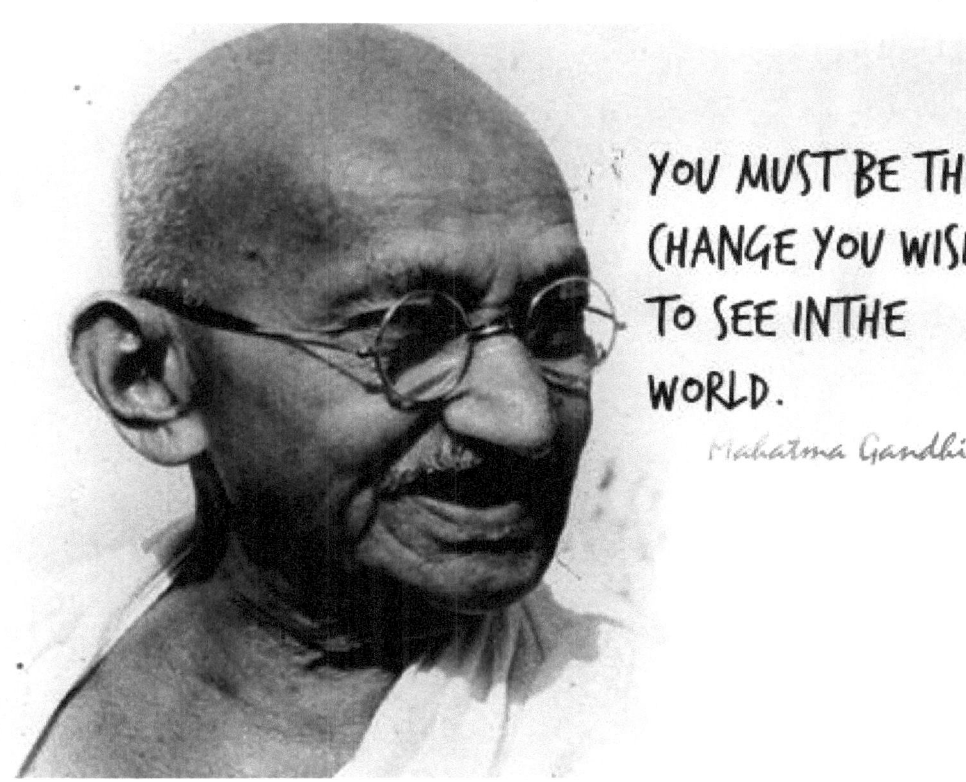

CHAPTER NINE

THE DASH

I read this poem that not only touched my heart, but also spoke volumes about how we should live our lives.

I read of a man who stood to speak.

At the funeral of a friend

He referred to the dates on her tombstone.

From the beginning to the end-

He noted that first came the date of her birth.

And spoke the following date with tears,

But he said what mattered most of all.

Was the dash between those years-

For that dash represents all the time

That she spent alive on earth.

And now only those who loved her.

Know what that little line is worth-

For it matters not how much we own.

The cars, the house, the cash

What matters is how we live and love?

And how we spend our dash-

So, think about this long and hard.

Are there things you would like to change?

For you never know how much time is left,

That can still be rearranged-

If we could just slow down enough

To consider what is true and real.

And always try to understand.

The way other people feel-

And be less quick to anger,

And show appreciation more.

And love the people in our lives.

Like we have never loved before-

If we treat each other with respect,

And more often wear a smile

Remembering that this special dash

Might only last a little while-

So, when your eulogy is being read.

With your life's actions to rehash

Would you be proud of the things they say?

About how you spent your dash?

I bet you are wondering what the point of that poem is, right? Is it really that important to put in this book? YES!! It is so important! Every day that I look in the mirror I wonder why I have wasted so much of my life. If I were to die today, I am not sure anyone would show up at my funeral unless it was to spit on my grave or to make sure I was Dead. I have not been the best person I could have been. I have disappointed many people during my life including myself and my four children.

Hence why I am writing this book. I want people to see how we can truly make a difference in one another's lives and how true kindness and understanding can and will make a difference. When I die, I want people to say I spent my dash in the best possible way. That I changed from the rotten selfish person I once was to someone who volunteered, who gave willingly to those who did not have, that taught from the heart so that people would understand. That I lived my life to serve others. That I was not afraid to pursue my dreams no matter how much work it took, or how others disapproved or said I would never accomplish anything. I want people to see that there is so much more to life than really meets the eye.

How have you been spending your dash? Are there any changes you would like to make? Are you the person God intended you to be? Are you making the best out of each day? Are you showing love and kindness to strangers?

I was watching how all these undocumented people are being separated from their children and how they were being contained in these cages. Little children who are emotionally confused about what is going on. One little boy looked at his dad and said, "Don't you love me anymore?" It literally broke my heart. That poor dad was devastated and beside himself, as he pulled away from his son. I cannot imagine that God is looking down at Trump with happiness at that point.

There are so many things that we as a nation just do not understand. Wouldn't we make our world a better place if we just gained knowledge and understanding? If we showed compassion for one another instead of selfishness? If we just stood up for what is right?

CHAPTER TEN

STRESS AND TRAUMA IN BABIES; HOW IT STARTS

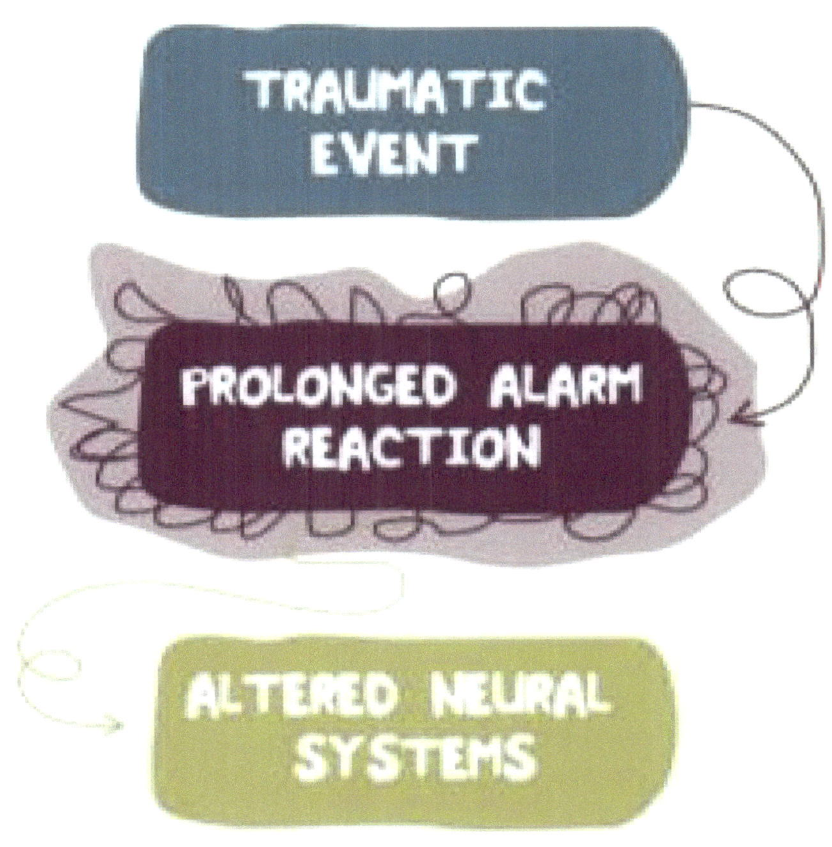

In the last chapter I spoke about the dash. How it represents the way we live our lives. Now knowing the way, we live our life affects so many people; not just ourselves I would like to share with you about how stress and trauma can start in babies and how it can affect their lived into adulthood. I was asked to do this parenting class and at first, I scoffed at taking it. My kids were grown, I more than likely would not be raising any more children, but I took it. So glad I did. It was so informational. I am so astounded at how things can affect us as humans. Did you know that a baby can become depressed? Or that they have that fight or flight capability? It is true. If a baby is fearful and goes into "fight mode" they cry continuously with out anyone being able to console them. Doctors used to call this "Failure to Thrive!" When people scream and yell, they are stressing and traumatizing that little baby. If they go into "flight mode" this is when a baby sleep entirely too much. Now we all know babies sleep a lot, but there are times when a baby will just check out. Emotional development starts in a baby from birth to 24 months. This is the "critical" window. If a baby is around all that fighting, screaming and abuse, chances are they will develop some serious mental health issues. If a baby or a young child is put into fight or flight mode, the limbic system will be enlarged by 30%. Which then causes the Cortex to shrink by 30%. The Cortex is the system that has the abstract thinking, planning, language creativity, problem solving and even the trust system. At 45 years old today, my trust system is nonexistent. The Limbic system is where the emotions, pain, hunger, thirst, pleasure, hormones, memory, and sexuality are contained. When the Limbic system is enlarged this means that things go a little hay wire. If the Cortex system is shrinking that means, there is not a lot of knowledge going on in that area. Causing a delay in the brain. It has been reported that 2.7 million children are reported by their caregivers to suffer from severe emotional or behavioral difficulties. These difficulties can persist through out development and lead to lifelong disabilities. Which can also include some severe mental health issues.

As a young child, I heard screaming, swearing, hitting and it caused severe fear in me. I would crawl under my bed and literally shake I was so scared. Always waiting for the other shoe to drop. Now as an adult, I get that feeling, but instead of hiding, I get angry. My fear is anger. I still shake, I still hide (behind that anger) I still struggle with trust.

When I first heard this in this parenting class, I was shocked. We always believe nothing like this affects babies. Especially for the rest of their lives. Damaged, for the rest of their lives.

Believe it or not it has now been proven that our brains do not stop developing when we are babies or young children, oh no, it continues into an adult's twenties.

Which now leads us to where all these addictions are coming from. Are you seeing a pattern here? Are you feeling a touch of guilt for judging those who have these addictions? I am not giving people excuses; I am just stating the facts. We all make our own choices, of course! We just make those choices by learning from what we know. How we have been taught.

I had one of those dad's who was a severe workaholic, was forever yelling or hitting someone. I was always walking on eggshells because I did not know what kind of mood he was in or what would set him off. There was no rhyme or reason to his moods. One minute he was laughing and joking, then the next he was beating the crap out of me, one of his wives or a stranger that had the audacity to pass him on the highway. We always heard how useless we were, or why he puts up with us. We were better off dead to him than alive. All my life I heard I would never amount to anything. I was always so scared that trying to focus on school was very hard for me. I was always so hyper vigilant, (still am today) that I did not have time to really take in what the teacher was saying. Which would only upset my dad even worse if I brought in anything less than an A. Now today, I am in college for Criminal Justice, and I cannot get anything less than an A. I will push myself to exhaustion or tears until I get that A. I received a B- and almost had a stroke. Started to cry and shake and flipping out. Immediately got into class and worked my tail off to change that B- to an A. I literally felt like I had committed murder getting that B-. It is a truly horrible feeling to feel like you will never be good enough no matter what you do. In my teenage years I was a horrible mess. Searching for someone to love me and accept me for me, yet I did not know who I truly was because I was always doing what others expected of me whether it was right or wrong. It got to the point I had no clue what I liked/disliked. Had no clue what I believed in. Finally, I succumbed over to alcohol and just started living my life out of control. Hurting others so they could not hurt me. Drinking constantly so I did not have to feel or be hyper vigilant. I was a mess.

All this stupid behavior than led me to reaching out to people who made me feel comfortable. People who did not care about themselves, who numbed their pain, and treated others like crap to make themselves feel better about THEMSELVES!! Which then led me down that destructive path even more. I was drinking so heavily my 'friends' found me passed out in the baseball field close to death from alcohol poisoning. To drugs that had me running naked down the street thinking hippos were chasing me. Being promiscuous just to find acceptance. I am so lucky death nor std's never found me.

Today after many years of counseling and many years of working on changing those voices, I now realize that these things do not have to define who I am. I never knew that I had a voice of my own. A voice that I want to use to help others. To help them realize earlier in life what I did not find out until later in life.

If I only knew the things then that I know now I would have been a very successful mother, friend, business associate and so much more. Do I have regrets today? Yes. Although I must admit that all my downfalls have helped me to overcome so much in my life. I believe that God brought me down this path for a reason. To help others and to first and foremost glorify God in all that he does and has done in my life.

I was reading this story about 'Children soldiers and the life they had to experience, and it broke my heart. Over the last twenty years, two million children have been used and killed in conflict. Over one million have been orphaned, over six million have been seriously injured or permanently disabled, and over ten million have been left with serious psychological trauma.

I found this picture on the internet and it broke my heart. This child had his innocence torn away from

him. These children were used to kill other human beings. They believed this was the right way of life.

This is what they knew. Impressionable children that should be learning, who should just be 'normal' kids. But this is how trauma works. It destroys every ounce of innocence in your mind and heart. You do not know the difference between right and wrong because you were not taught right from wrong. You lean on those of higher authority. You trust them to guide you down the right path. You put your faith into these people that are teaching you how to live your life.

There was this young lady who was in prison with me and so was her mother. One day I heard the two of them talking and the mom said to her daughter, "I'm so sorry I had you stealing for me to fulfill my addictions." This young lady was in prison for stealing for her mother. I was so sad. This girl had been stealing for her mother since she was two years old. How was she to know that what her mother was having her do was wrong? She did not until it was to late. Just like these children's soldiers do not know what they are doing is wrong.

Then the next step is the shame you feel when you realize you do not have the same lifestyle as others. The way people look at you, or whisper or make fun of you. You begin to grow up and realize, "hmmm...something isn't right here." Why does this person look so happy? Why doesn't he/she always have bruises or broken bones? Why does this person's mom/dad spend so much time with them? You start thinking something unnatural is going on in THEIR lives when all along it has been in your own life. Once I got out of prison, I met this man and his daughter. He treated his daughter like she was his little wife. He would share his day with his 11-year-old as if he were sharing with his significant other. He would share his happiness or sorrow with her. He would share jokes with her that were wildly inappropriate. My first thought was this guy has abused his daughter sexually. I confronted him about it and the look of hurt on his face was horrible. I then thought more about it and realized I was putting my issues into his relationship with his daughter. Now do I agree that a father should be sharing his sorrows and his tough day with his 11-year-old? No, I believe there are certain boundaries, but this does not mean he is doing bad things to her sexually. See how you just do not know and how your life affects every decision? Makes you doubt others. How you view so much as unnatural?

The atrocities that you endure affect every aspect of your life. The way you think or do not think. I remember being in like fourth grade and I could not see the chalk board. I thought I was just stupid, and I was terrified to tell my teacher I could not see. What if she told my dad? So, I failed fourth grade because I could not understand half my classes. Well, that just made matters worse for me. I then had to listen to my dad tell me what an embarrassment I was and how stupid I was as he was beating me near death.

Trauma is one of those demons that sucks the life and innocence out of a person and then people wonder why the prison systems are so full. People view crime as deviant behavior that violates prevailing norms, cultural standards teaching how humans ought to behave normally. This approach considers the complex realities surrounding the concept of crime and seeks to understand how ever changing social, political, psychological, and economic conditions may affect the definitions of crime and the form of law enforcement made by society. This should have been happening a very long time ago. If people would have just taken the time to LISTEN to me, BELIEVE me and CARE for me they probably would have saved a lot of MY innocent victims. I have many! There are banks who entrusted me with bank accounts, and I constantly bounced checks. I had no clue how to have a bank account, how to budget it. I forged checks in the amount of $400 from a landlord who was kind enough to rent his home out to me. Here I was 18 years old living in Baileys Harbor, Wi. The most beautiful tourist area around, in a beautiful home and I did not know how to be respectful to the owner who entrusted me with his home. I stole from a T-shirt company that entrusted me with a job. I could have been so much more, but I did not know. I think back today how I AM smart enough. I could have done anything with my life. There are victims that I have that I never met face to face, but I did prison time for because of people I surrounded myself with. I made a complete mess out of my life, and messes for others.

So many innocent victims all because of trauma, addictions, and mental health issues. When does it stop? I was watching the news and there was this young man who shot quite a few people in Toronto, Canada. What made him do this? What was his life? Was he abused? Did he suffer from mental health issues? These are the questions that need to be asked BEFORE something serious happens. Not after. We need to start looking deeper into people's hidden secrets. Start to take notice. See that young man who is a complete loner? What is going on in his life? Because normal children do not hide away unless something is seriously wrong. Start to take notice, because what is going to happen to the generation of our grandchildren and their children? If we do not start taking notice people are going to destroy this world as we know it.

CHAPTER ELEVEN

CARING ABOUT THE NEEDS OF OTHERS

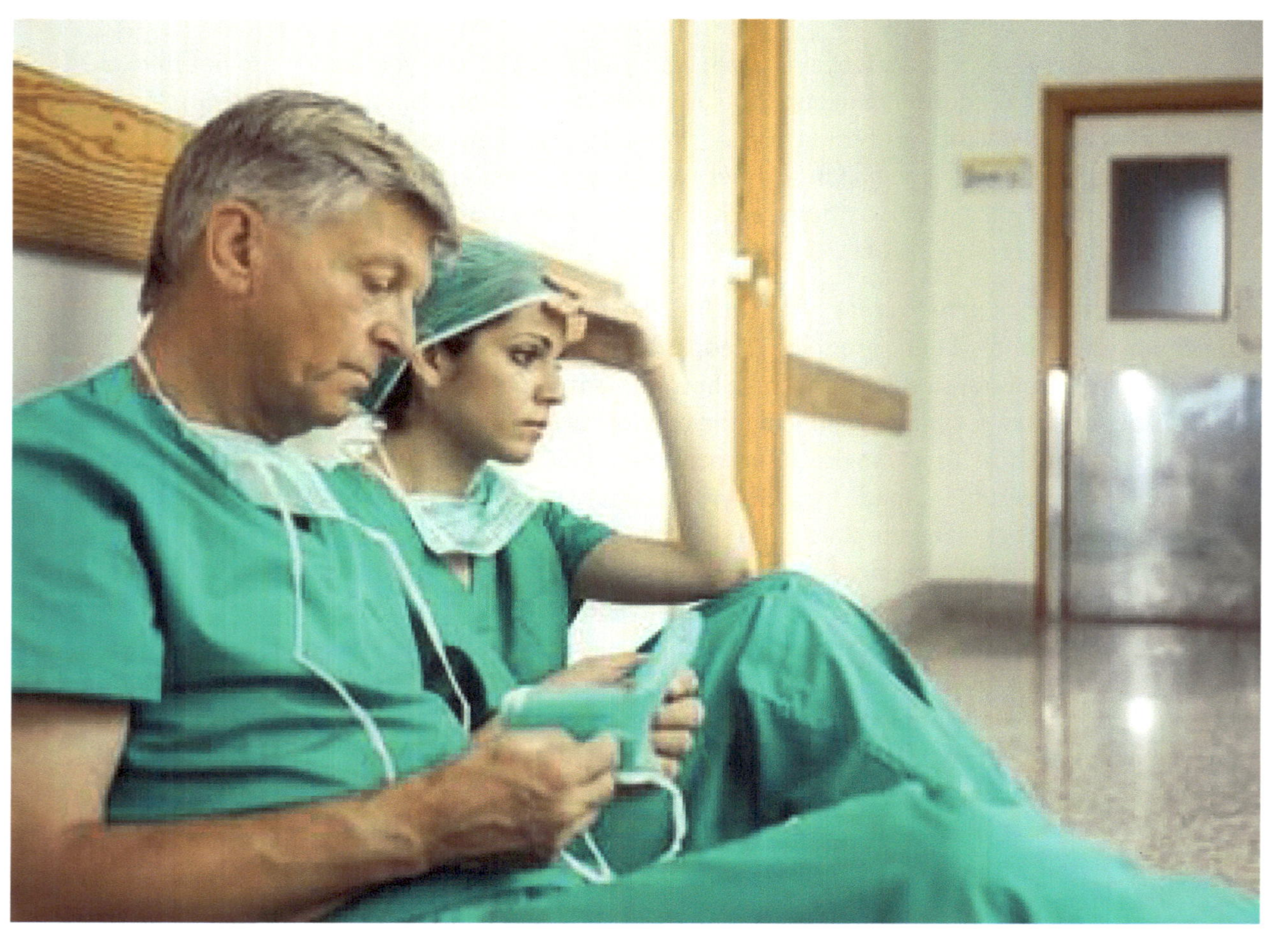

Can you explain to me why it takes a person to come to prison to find out how sick they really are? Why aren't children being tested for mental health issues so maybe we can save them and many victims the problems of addiction? Why are we not teaching children that it is okay to find that one person to reach out to when they are in trouble? Why are we so afraid of what others think?

Even as adults we are afraid to mention things that are bothering us. We would rather just complain about everyday things like, the sun is too hot, or there is no sun, what a dreary day! Or whatever we may complain about on the daily. We are never happy with what is going on in our lives, so why not do something about it? Why hide?

I was thinking about Robin Williams and what a great actor he was. You would never believe he was suffering from alcohol or drug addictions or from a mental health illness such as depression.

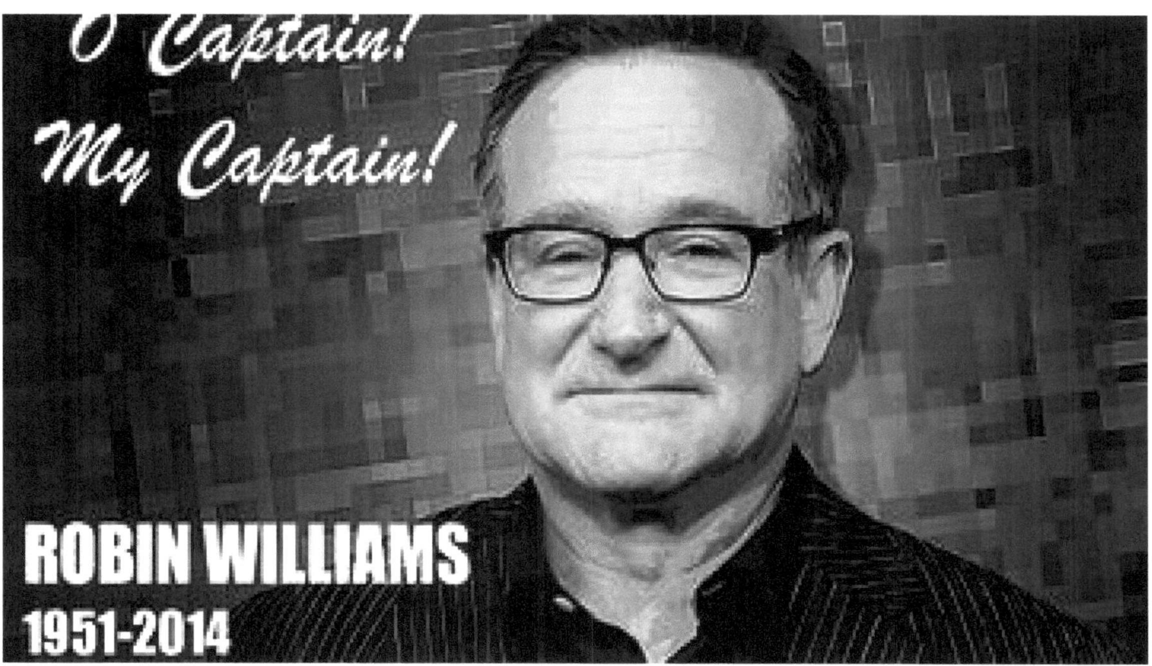

Robin Williams checked himself into a Rehabilitation Center in Minnesota right before he committed suicide. Watching him all my life I always BELIEVED he was genuinely happy. He never portrayed himself in any other way. He was compassionate, kind, happy, adoring, adored, laughing, joking. An all-around great guy!! How many of you were shocked when he took his own life? How many of you were rocked to your very core? I know I was. To this day, I get choked up thinking about him. The loneliness he must have felt inside his heart, knowing he was portrayed one way, but was TRULY a different way.

This is what mental health does to a person. It shames you, takes away your self-esteem, and your self-confidence. You begin to believe that something is fundamentally wrong with you, but you have no clue what it is. You begin to avoid the pain with any addiction that you can hide behind. It can be drugs, alcohol, gambling, food, sex or anything that you can shield yourself behind. Trust me though, you can only hide for so long before all hell breaks loose, and you only have two paths to take. The right or wrong way. I am not talking about right or wrong for others, but for yourself. Robin Williams right way was taking his life.

When this does not work the hopelessness kicks in and there is just no light at the end of the tunnel. All darkness! All devastation. Life as you know it becomes too unbearable. You convince yourself that the world sees you as one way when you are really seen in another or not seen at all. In the eyes of the world, people may be highly functional, when you are anxious, driven, angry and often depressed. And NOONE knows it, until it is to late.

I was reading this book and it was talking about the symptoms of depression. I am guessing after I describe each symptom you will say to yourself, hmm...I have felt like that a couple of times in my life. If you feel this way imagine how those who have been diagnosed with manic depression must feel. Then have no clue why they are feeling this way before being diagnosed. Some symptoms are losing interest or pleasure in things that used to bring you immense joy. Feeling this way almost every day. Significant weight loss/gain. Disturbed sleep or to much sleep. Feeling worthless. Feeling like no one gives a damn about you. Including yourself. Having issues with the ability to think or concentrate. Being frustrated because things that were once easy are now so hard to do.

I suffer from manic depression. Never knew I did until a few years ago. Never understood why I felt the way I did. Today, I suffer significantly, and I now realize why. When I first got out of prison I had so many goals. So many plans. It was so important to me to use the things I had learned to make a difference in my life. In others lives! I had my one year, three-year, five year and ten-year goals and plans. Guess what not one thing has happened that I had planned for myself. Instead of staying single, I got involved with this man after two months of release. I thought he was awesome, kind, caring, hardworking, trustworthy, great father and I could go on and on, but I will not. Well, after three months of being with him I found out he was going out to lunch with his ex-girlfriend, asking her to kiss him and come back to his home to mess around. Do you think I left? Nope! I believed him that he would never do it again. Guess what, turns out he did do it again. Told another ex he loved her and wanted to be with her, while begging me to stay. Did I leave then? Nope. Believed him AGAIN. Three years later I am still with him. Has anything been different? I am not sure. He is meaner, lazier, I am not allowed to say anything without him getting an attitude or saying stuff like I do not care about anyone, but myself, Him acting like he can say or do what ever he wants. He still treats his daughter like she is his little wife. I always feel like I am beneath her and everyone else. So why do I stay right? Because my depression is so great that I cannot even hold my head up. I cry every day. I beg him to show me respect. I scream and yell, and cry. Does it do any good? Not at all. I always thought he changed. Then I realized it was not him that changed but me. He has always been this mean; I am better than you bully. I have changed because now I scream, yell, cry, give up. Then he will be nice to me and I will fall for it then the cycle goes on again. The difference is now I KNOW what abuse looks like. Now I KNOW what depression looks like. Am I perfect? Oh no! Not even close! But I feel like I am a damn good woman! First off, I stayed when most women would have left him the first time he cheated. Second, I keep a very clean home, pay all the bills, love his daughter as if she is my own flesh and blood, do all the grocery shopping, try to build a home inside and out. I do not cheat, lie, steal, sneak or do anything along those lines. So, am I perfect? No, but I am a damn good woman!!! I am not saying he is a bad guy, but what he is not what I want. I want a man that likes to communicate, do things as a family, not sit around night and day. I want a man that I can share my life with my feelings with, without feeling like I am bothering him. I have taken interest in things that he loves like football, wrestling stuff like that. I want him to value me as much. Take an interest in what I like to do or enjoy! I want a happy life. So why do I stay? Because of my depression. I KNOW in my heart I am a good woman TODAY, but my past hinders me in leaving. Do I want to start all over? Do I want to get to know someone all over just to find out that what they are selling me is fake again? Do I want to start all over again? The feeling of worthlessness and hopelessness keeps me from leaving. My fear keeps me from leaving. My heart knows better but my mind is my enemy in all things. This is what depression does.

There are many treatments for manic depression but how do people know this if they never had any training? Have not learned about depression? Have not learned the signs and symptoms of depression? What is worse is that there are other mental health issues that look like depression but are not. Like Bi-polar. Attention Deficit, ADHD. There are so many things' people can have and not even realize it or understand it. I was 19 years old and there was this man and woman who had a seven-year-old son who was completely out of control. He would slap his mother, scream, throw tantrums, run out into the street, you name it, and this kid did it. The mother took him to the doctor, and they just assumed he had some 'extra energy'. Until he raped a younger boy...my son. It was then they decided to diagnose him with ADHD. They put him on Ritalin, and he was totally different. Ritalin was originally prescribed as an antidepressant for adults. This is a stimulant from the family of amphetamines. After a lot of research, they found out that Ritalin blocks the dopamine transporters and so preventing reuptake of dopamine back into the releasing neuron. Which then gives the patient a chance to settle down. To be able to think before reacting. It was scary because that child was on his way to prison, and no one had any idea what was wrong with him.

This is the way that mental health illnesses go. People don't reach out because they are A.) to young B.) they don't know anything is wrong until its to late, C.) They are told they are just making excuses D.) They are embarrassed or afraid to say anything. This is very sad if you ask me! Every day is a constant struggle for myself because I AM learning new skills that I should have known about when I was a little kid, not at 42-45 years old.

Imagine the lives we could each save if we just started 'noticing others' instead of being so focused on ourselves, or afraid.

"IT IS A VERY DELICATE JOB TO FORGIVE A MAN, WITHOUT LOWERING HIM IN HIS ESTIMATION, AND YOURS TOO."

JOSH BILLINGS 1818-1885

CHAPTER TWELVE

DEPENDANCE AND WHAT IT LOOKS LIKE

As we have discussed earlier in this book there are different forms of dependencies. There is the alcohol dependency which has been around since the cave-man days. For more than six thousand years people have been producing alcohol from plant life and using it to feel better. This is the ultimate reason. People drink to feel better, to have a good time, to drown their sorrows, to feel better socially, to feel better financially (look at me I can afford to drink whatever or whenever I want), to feel less anger, hurt. There IS a rhyme and reason to why people drink. People use alcohol as a catalyst for celebrations, birthdays, graduations, football games, negotiations, you name it they use it.

An alcoholic is someone who has become so solidly dependent on alcohol that their brain believes this person will surely die without it. That they cannot do normal everyday activities without being drunk. Then they have to drink more to reach the level of 'happiness' so the cycle continues to go. That is why people reach for the vodka bottle like others reach for the coffee pot, or a bottle of water. FYI coffee can also be an addiction.

I have heard people say if a person wants to quit drinking all they must do is quit. Little do people know though, that recovering from years of drinking is tough. You go through withdrawals that can cause severe pain and agony. You become shaky, jittery, sweaty, go through hallucinations, which can then lead to delirium. Which means you are flat out of your mind. Recovering from years of heavy consumption is very tough both mentally and physically. Instead of judging people maybe try to find some compassion in your heart, do an intervention with them, get them to a rehabilitation center. Do something to save this person's life instead of getting angry or using "TOUGH LOVE". Tough love my foot!! That is an excuse to bury your head in the sand and not notice what the other person is doing.

Psychology is an academic and applied discipline involving the phenomenological and scientific study of mental processes and behavior. Psychologists study such concepts as perception, cognition, emotion, personality, behavior, interpersonal relationships, and the individual and collective unconscious. Psychology also refers to the application of such knowledge to various spheres of human activity including issues related to daily life- family, education, and work. The treatment of mental health problems. Psychology attempts to understand the role these functions play in social behavior and in social dynamics, while incorporating the underlying physiological and neurological processes into its conceptions of mental functioning. Psychology includes many sub fields of study and application concerned with such areas as human developments, sports, health, industry, media, law. Having a psychologist do an intervention with you or your loved one is usually the first step in a very long process. But well worth it if it means saving someone's life. Please do not overlook that loved one who really struggles with addiction.

I had a fiancé' who was 22 years older than me, and he once told me, "I can't imagine going one day let alone one hour without a drink, let alone twenty years". When he told me that I was ten ways to Sunday…angry! I looked at him and said, "so alcohol is more important than me or our relationship? In the end it was his alcoholism that destroyed us. Not because I gave up on him, but he gave up on himself. Alcohol was just too important to him. I could not give him what he needed the most…. ALCOHOL!! Unfortunately, to this day I wonder if he is still alive or if he killed himself or someone else. Maybe he is back in prison. I just do not know. A great guy he was with all the qualities of a saint until he got drunk and then he had the qualities of the devil himself. It was just way to overwhelming for me. For him as well, He wanted to quit but did not have the foggiest idea how to do it, and I sure did not know nor at that time did I have the patience or the coping skills or knowledge to be able to help myself let alone someone struggling with addiction.

This is the problem with our society today. We are so busy with our own lives that we do not have time to take notice of others. The more understanding that we have the better off our world would be. The better off our children and their children would be. Isn't it time to quit hiding and educate ourselves so we can help our son, daughter, mom or dad? Not judge them and belittle them? So, we can make our world a better place?

Back in 1985 Michael Jackson and Lionel Richie produced by Quincy Jones and Michael Omartian for the album We are the World. Whenever I hear this song, it propels me to be a better person, to work harder for this world.

The chorus went something like this…excuse me if I do not get all the words exactly right but you will get the gist of it.

We are the world.

We are the children.

We are the ones who make for a brighter day.

So, let us start giving.

There is a chance we are taking.

Taking our own lives

Its true we will make a brighter day.

Just you and me!

How true is this? If just one person comes together for a purpose of helping those who struggle with mental illness or addictions imagine the possibilities! Friends, this book is all about making a difference in the world. By not being afraid to show ALL of ME. To not be afraid of all the judgements out there, but to take a leap of faith that my story will help at least one person.

There is so much tragedy in the world today. Imagine, being fifteen years old and having a man in his 50's tries to rape you, and you find the closest thing to get him away from you and you kill him with a few well-placed aims to the head and he dies. You do not tell a single soul because you are terrified. Will they believe me? Will they believe I was scared? So instead of turning to the police who you have been raised to hate all your life, you run. Five years later the police catch up with you. Now you are 20 years old, and you get sentenced to 19 years in prison and 20 years on parole. What would you do? This is what Fear is doing to people. Now I am pretty sure while you are reading this book from the love seat in your home. Snow falling outside or maybe the sun is out on a beautiful August day, but either way you are safe and content in your home with your family and your first inclination is to say well of course I would just call the police. Why? Because you were taught to believe that the police are safe. They are there to serve and protect. You were taught to believe in the justice system. That they will fully investigate the crime for what it is. Oh, did I mention this fifteen-year-old girl was black as well? The reason I bring all this up is most people who are currently sitting in prison have a lot of odds stacked against them, drug dealers, drug users, violent offenders, people like THEM are liars, users, abusers. No, not true! Everybody has a story! It is whether you take the time to listen, intervene and believe. I was molested from the age of two on. I was told this was normal. Not to say anything. Some people have been told that the police are bad. I mean look at the news today! That is a whole other book! Some have horrible mental illnesses. Some people have been raised from an infant on by criminals themselves. These fears do not excuse people, but they do show that fear is very overwhelming.

Are you afraid of spiders? How do you react if a spider suddenly drops from the ceiling onto your arm? Well, let me tell you, I am terrified of spiders and if one dropped onto MY arm, I am going to act super dramatic. Why? Because I was taught at a young age that spiders are dangerous. This is MY true reaction. For every action there is a reaction and for every reaction there is an action. We all have three sets of overly emotional tendencies. Flight, fight or fright. EVERYONE has experienced these emotions at one point in their life. Others experience them every day of their life. You tend to do things out of fear. Some will experience these more than others but at the end of the day we all still experience them. This is how someone who has been traumatized will act. Heck, if you get in a severe accident, spend months in the hospital, are you going to jump right into another car? Heck no! You will feel scared, apprehensive, not sure of yourself or other drivers. That is because our limbic system in our brain contains our emotions. It has now been red lighted, and we are going to fear things. This is our nature. We were designed by God to be this way!

Does this cause you to be sympathetic? Compassionate? Maybe more empathetic? More understanding? This is how we need to be, have some understanding for others the way we would want understanding in our lives.

"THERE ARE TWO WAYS OF SPREADING LIGHT; TO BE THE CANDLE OR THE MIRROR THAT REFLECTS IT.' EDITH NEWBOLD WHARTON 1862-1937

CHAPTER THIRTEEN

WHAT IS POST TRAUMATIC STRESS DISORDER?

In the prior chapter we talked about fear and before that mental health disorder. Now I would like to talk about Post Traumatic Stress Disorder also known as P.T.S.D. Way back in the day P.T.S.D. was attributed only to the soldiers. Now we have come to find out it is an exposure to a stressful event. Like watching your comrade getting killed or being in a natural disaster. I was reading about PTSD and it indicated some potentially traumatic events and I wanted to share them with you. Now there are man made situations that can cause PTSD which can be controlled by others. If we just treated one another the way, we want to be treated we would not have to experience these things. Some man-made situations are rape, incest, forced nudity, pornography, inappropriate touching, fondling or kissing. There is also beating on someone, kicking them, battering them, choking them tying them up, stalking or forcing to eat or drink something. There is also the emotional aspect of PTSD. Which includes but is not limited to isolation, belittling, telling someone they will never amount to anything, bullying with words, threats to leave, threats of suicide. I remember how my dad would always tell me, "One day you are going to find me hanging from the ceiling!" To this day I get very uncomfortable walking into a room for the first time. Intimidation, neglect, minimizing abuse, blaming said abuse on the victim, controlling, destroying property, killing/ abusing pets are just some of the emotional aspects of which can cause PTSD.

I read this book called "A CHILD CALLED IT" True story by Dave Pelzer. Let me tell you this child endured so much it literally made me sick to my stomach. If you have never read this true story, you need to. One example I want to use of emotional and physical abuse is when Dave was being starved by his mother so he would go to school and steal other kids' lunches. One time he was caught by the teacher and she call his mother unaware of the abuse he was enduring at home. When Dave got home that night his mother made him eat a bunch of hot dogs and then when he threw up, she made him eat his throw up. If you think this is bad, his life only got worse. I will not spoil it for you. READ THE BOOK!!!

The great thing is that he was able to use his experience to write about his abuse. To help others become aware. When someone first mentioned I should write a book about my life, I was disgusted! No way, that is private! I was astounded anyone would even suggest it. Then I thought about what changed my life, it was finally realizing I was not alone, that others had experienced some of the same things I had, and some had experienced worse.

Anyway, sorry, let me get back to these manmade situations. There is hi-jacking someone's car, an airplane, bombings, shootings, being held hostage, cult abuse and on and on. Do you see how many things there are that could cause PTSD and imagine how many people are walking around with these fears and do not even realize that it is a mental disease, it could literally hold you back from doing something that could change their lives for the better or could lead you into unsafe situations. Now there are also Unintentional accidents that can cause P.T.S.D. I will not list all of them, but you will be surprised at a couple of them. There is Industrial situations like when a crane crash down. I just seen this on the news a few years ago where the crane crashed down right onto the highway. Imagine how many people were affected by this. Not just where the crane came down, but the accidents that happened due to this crane coming down. Oil rigs that catch on fire, boats catching on fire, commercial boats sinking. Then you have P.T.S.D that is caused by natural disasters like Tornadoes, Hurricanes, Floods, Drought, Famine and so on. When I first got out of prison I went to Appleton, Wisconsin to have breakfast with a friend and then we went and worked out. Just as I was about to head home, a Tornado hit. It happened so fast. I pulled into Pick n Save first and the wind was so strong the carts were literally flying around the parking lot. So, I went down to the gas station and when I attempted to get out of the car, my glasses were flung off my face and the car was rocking dramatically. I finally made my way into the gas station and all hell hit. As soon as I see dark clouds I freak out and say a Tornado is coming. Is this irrational? Possibly, but having stressed induced situations happen to you leave a long-lasting fear in you which is identified as P.T.S.D.

With trauma and abuse you tend to have more severe P.T.S.D. Long lasting effects that can potentially ruin your life. Because of my abusers I have no friends, I have a hard time going into the grocery store alone, because I have such bad panic attacks. I am unable to do many fun things that impact my family. The worst of it is when I get into that panic, my go to is fight and boy do I get mad. You would be like wow she is overreacting, but I am not present in the moment. I am literally back in the past fighting for my life.

Fear is not an easy thing to deal with. So have respect for people and take the time to get to know them instead of just judging them. It may also help you to deal with your own fear and understand 'why' people may act the way they do.

CHAPTER FOURTEEN

FEAR AND HOW IT AFFECTS YOUR WELL-BEING

Fear is a very dark and lonely place. Growing up I was always taught to never show fear because fear is a sign of weakness. When I was getting harmed by my dad and I would show fear it would just make matters worse. Or if I cried. So, I grew up never showing fear. Being stoic in all things. For many years I did not show fear, nor did I cry, and it made me so reckless. I mean where do you go with that fear that is inside you, but do not show it? Just stuff it away.

Now before we go into where we put our fears lets talk about fear as an emotion. On Wikipedia I was doing some research and I found this small yet very informative article on what emotion is. I really liked it because it states in it how emotions come with bodily changes. If someone is coming at you with a baseball bat and he is cursing and shouting at you, you WILL feel fear. It is out of your control. What you do with that fear is a completely different story.

All my life I was one of those people that would not show my fear, or so I thought, instead of fear I would get so angry, and I would ask myself why am I so angry? I did not realize that anger was the secondary emotion.

One day while in prison, I was standing in the medication line and there was a door to the left of me. I happened to look down and I saw a spider crawling under the door. It was so big it left a shadow. The gasp that came flying out of my mouth scared the others that were in line with me. They asked what that was for and I said, "there's the biggest spider that just crawled under the door. The girl in front of me started to laugh and she said, "aww the big tough Nikki is afraid of an itty-bitty spider." I exploded right then and there at her. I yelled, swore, said things to hurt her. To make her feel as bad as I did. One of the staff members asked me to step in the other room and he pointed out while it was not right for the girl to laugh at me over my fear it was not right for me to lash out at her like that. He said, "why are you so angry?" I could not answer him at first. He then said," do you think maybe you were afraid, and you needed to get that fear out in any way you could?" I did not know where to go with that, so I just cried. I was so completely devastated and unaware of how terrified I truly was. All these new feelings were different. Fear, crying all new.

Since then, I have been trying to learn more about different emotions. Again, I am now 45 years old, and you would think I would understand the different emotions. I do not. I still struggle with that secondary emotion ANGER every time I am fearful. I am also learning that it is ok to feel other emotions. I still struggle with that anger mask as well. If I look angry people will not come near me and then I do not have to deal with anyone.

Affect is a synonym for emotion; this term is used when the emotional experience has been qualified or quantified. There are different displays of emotion. Affect display is an external display of emotion such as facial expression, body posture or voice quality. A person's disposition is referring to a person's characteristic, a tendency to react to certain classes of situations with a certain emotion. So, if you are at a bank and the bank is full you can gather that every person is going to react differently if an armed robber walks in. Some will show their fear with anger, others with sobbing, some may try to be the hero. Then others will just remain calm and do as they are told.

The James-Lange Theory is so simplistic to most, but for others you may not know what exactly you are feeling is a moment. William James in the article, "What is an emotion?" (Mind,9,1884:188-205) argued that emotional experience is largely due to the experience of bodily changes. These changes might be visceral, postural, or facially expressive. What if your body reacts to all emotions in the same way though? How can you ascertain exactly what is going on inside of you? Therefore, it is so important to analyze what is going on, what symptoms you are feeling inside of your body, and to figure out exactly what you are feeling so you can handle a situation appropriately. I have been handling every situation with either joy or anger. Very high or very low. This leads yourself and others to confusion. My fiancé' will hurt my feelings, and instead of letting him know he hurt my feelings I get super angry and start acting crazy. I struggle big time with this. I try to do self-talk, but I am so bound up in that anger that it really does not go anywhere except to an argument.

I seen a picture of Adolf Hitler and I was quite surprised at the regal handsome look he had. It got me to thinking of how he was raised and what traumas he must have experienced as a child to have that cold, murderous, unfeeling anger inside of him. I was surprised to find out that he suffered from severe depression and suicidal tendencies. When he was eleven years old his younger brother, Edmund died from the measles. This dramatically affected Hitler. The once overly confident outgoing, excelling student now became morose, detached and sullen, and was constantly fighting with his father and teachers. There seemed to be a lot of upheavals in Adolf's life. His father wanted him to go to a certain school that Adolf did not want to attend. He wanted to be an artist, but his father was against it. His mother than died. It was one thing after another for Adolf. Unfortunately, in those days they did not know what depression was, or what even suicidal tendencies represented. Hence, the Adolf Hitler we have come to know. Do you think maybe if they understood suicidal tendencies, depression or PTSD the world would be a different place today where Adolf Hitler is concerned? I do. I believe the world would be different all together if there would have been understanding or knowledge.

I know when I look at my life and how all these different emotions were displayed and how such a huge part in how I reacted and acted I know things would have been different in my own life.

All my life I have been afraid of putting myself out there. What will people think? How will they treat me? Will they judge me based on my mental health issues? I still struggle with these thoughts. The difference today is I now understand what Mental Health is, what trauma and abuse is, how none of that is my fault and how just by educating myself and becoming a different person with a lot of hard work I can make a change. Not just in myself, but that one person who has no clue what is going on in their life, what they are feeling or what they are experiencing. If I can help one person to take a different path than I did, all my trials and tribulations will have been worth it. If I can help one person know that being molested was not their fault, all my molestations will have been worth it.

Thank you for allowing me to share my story. Please feel free to reach out to me at any time!

Nicole Klotter

klottern@gmail.com

FEAR

Don't be afraid of fear

Because fear is afraid of itself

You give into fear when you doubt yourself

Fear makes you a complete opposite of yourself

Draining every bit of confidence your body has left

Fear tricks you of your potential

Wiping away your credentials

A life ruled by fear is life without hope

Of course people are going to have raining days

But with fear, everyday you will have your droughts

Be confident and put your head up high

How can fear overtake you when you're looking at the

Beautiful clouds high in the sky

rico graham